Instrum
in the

OR THE

GREEK VERB PSALLO

PHILOLOGICALLY AND HISTORICALLY EXAMINED

TOGETHER WITH A

FULL DISCUSSION of KINDRED MATTERS

RELATING TO

MUSIC IN CHRISTIAN WORSHIP

———

By M. C. KURFEES

Associate Editor of the Gospel Advocate
Author of "Walking by Faith," Etc.

———

GOSPEL ADVOCATE COMPANY
Nashville, Tennessee
1975

Published by Gospel Advocate Co.
P.O. Box 150
Nashville, TN 37202
www.gospeladvocate.com

First Published: 1911

ISBN 0-89225-500-5

CONTENTS.

CONTENTS.

PREFACE.

This book is the outgrowth of an incident in connection with a class in New Testament Exegesis. During the winter of 1906-'7, while the author was conducting a class of young preachers through parts of the New Testament, the Greek verb *psallo* (ψάλλω) came up for consideration. Questions on the meaning of this word and collateral subjects became too numerous for proper treatment during the hour of recitation; and hence, to avoid interference with the regular work of the class, it was agreed to appoint a special day at the close of the term, when any questions on these matters, which the members of the class might wish to present, would be duly considered. In the hope of covering much of the ground on which light was desired, the author prepared a paper on PSALLO (ψάλλω), which was read to the class and others on the appointed day, and was followed, as per previous agreement, with a free and easy discussion of such questions as had not been answered by the document read. Much of the matter contained in Chapters I.-VII. of this work was presented in the paper prepared for that occasion.

Numerous calls were made for its publication, but it was decided to make some additions to it before giving it to the public. Continued research convinced the author that, notwithstanding the repeated discussion of the music question in different ages prior to the Reformation of the nineteenth century and the general discussion of it by leading reformers forty years ago, still there was no single work, known to him, which contained either an exhaustive treatment of the term *psallo* (ψάλλω), or a general consensus of testimony which could be properly regarded as a book of reference on the subject. He was, therefore, encouraged to prosecute his research in the different fields of evidence, keeping constantly in view the aim to make the work a ready and reliable book of reference. No pains have been spared to put within easy reach of the reader all that is necessary to enable one to see how the subject has been viewed by Christian scholars in every age from the beginning of the Christian era to the present time. Hence, in a few hours and within a small compass, the reader can here find what would otherwise require much time and the reading of many volumes. Young preachers and all others, who have not had the time to go over the different fields of evidence, will find it a convenient and labor-saving book of reference.

As to the claim sometimes made that the majority of people regard the question as a "dead issue," we respectfully observe: 1. An issue over which the people of God are constantly clashing and which is causing division and alienation among them, cannot properly be termed a "dead issue," but this is strictly true of the issue over instrumental music in Christian worship. 2. The *discussion* of it, the author is well aware, is shut out of a part of the journalistic press, not because it is a "dead issue," but because those who control the press in such cases, for reasons satisfactory to themselves, *do not want it discussed;* but on precisely the same principle and for the same reason, infant baptism, pouring and sprinkling for baptism, burning incense, auricular confession, and many other perversions of the Bible and departures from it are called "dead issues" with a part of the journalistic press closed against their discussion. 3. As to "majorities," Galileo and the Copernican system of astronomy were in an obscure and despised minority at the opening of the seventeenth century, and the latter was such a "dead issue" with the majority that the brilliant Italian philosopher was sent to prison for his views under sentence of papal authority, but the great principle for which he stood ultimately triumphed and rules in the world of astronomy to-day. Man often places on the "*Index Expurgatorius*" what God wants "proclaimed upon the housetops." The simplicity of the divine order set forth in the New Testament is the same in all ages, and its friends cannot cease to defend it because of the vacillating popular sentiment of any particular age.

For the advantage of certain readers, it has seemed proper, in some instances, to give Greek words and sometimes a Greek passage in full, but these, as a rule, are either inclosed in parentheses, or placed in a footnote where they will not materially interfere with the English reader.

The author gratefully acknowledges his indebtedness to friends too numerous to mention by name, who have urged and encouraged the preparation of this work. He is especially indebted to his friend and coworker, J. W. Shepherd, of Nashville, Tenn., Office Editor of the Gospel Advocate, for valuable assistance in the collection of historic documents and in the preparation of the Index.

With the devout and earnest prayer to God that this book may be instrumental in maintaining intact the order of worship revealed in the New Testament, it is now committed to the mission and destiny to which it may be allotted by His overruling Providence.   M. C. KURFEES.

Louisville, Ky., January 31, 1911.

Instrumental Music in the Worship.

CHAPTER I.

Preliminary Considerations.

Before entering directly into an examination of the main question claiming attention on this occasion,* I wish to present, first of all, a brief historic outline which, it is hoped, will prepare us for a better appreciation of all the facts, *pro* and *con,* which are involved in the discussion. It would not be practical, nor is it necessary here, to elaborate, in detail, all the statements in such an outline, but it is deemed sufficient, for all essential purposes, merely to note such preliminaries as will properly present and en-

---

*The *occasion* here referred to was a special day which, for the accommodation of a class of young men in New Testament exegesis, had been set apart to consider any questions which they might wish to ask on the mooted instrumental-music controversy, and particularly on the meaning of the Greek word *psallo* (ψάλλω). Much of Chapters I. to VII. of this work was prepared by the author and presented, substantially, in a document read to the class on that occasion, and was followed, as per previous agreement, by the consideration of such additional questions as had not been anticipated and met in the document read. The interview proved to be both pleasant and profitable. See the Preface.

able us to see, in a clearer light, the real merits of the question before us. Hence, while the following pages are occupied, in a large measure, with facts and principles relating to the history and meaning of a single word, yet we deem it proper, before entering directly upon the main line of argument, to invite attention to the following facts:

I. THERE IS NOT A SOLITARY MENTION OF INSTRUMENTAL MUSIC IN THE WORSHIP OF ANY NEW TESTAMENT CHURCH, NOR IN ANY INSTANCE OF CHRISTIAN WORSHIP THROUGHOUT THE APOSTOLIC AGE.

Now, if there were no other proof in connection with the whole controversy, this fact of itself, so far as the wish to occupy infallibly safe ground is concerned, would be entirely sufficient for all thoughtful and unbiased minds.

II. ITS FIRST APPEARANCE IN HISTORY IN CHRISTIAN WORSHIP WAS ABOUT THE SIXTH CENTURY, A.D., THE EXACT DATE OF ITS INTRODUCTION VARYING IN DIFFERENT LOCALITIES AND ACCORDING TO DIFFERENT AUTHORITIES, BUT THERE WAS NO GENERAL ATTEMPT TO INTRODUCE IT TILL AFTER THE EIGHTH CENTURY.

It should be noted here that the claim has been set up by some authorities in modern times that it was used in the worship, though with opposition, as early as the close of the second century; but if this claim should ever become authenticated, the opposition which it is alleged to have encountered would be a strong point against the lawfulness of the practice. The authority sometimes claimed in support of its early use is Clement of Alexandria, whose case the reader will find carefully examined in Chapter XII. of this work.

III. INFANT BAPTISM, THE SUBSTITUTION OF POURING AND SPRINKLING FOR IMMERSION, THE BURNING OF INCENSE, AND AURICULAR CONFESSION, WERE ALL INTRODUCED BEFORE INSTRUMENTAL MUSIC, AND BY THE SAME AUTHORITY.

None of these innovations upon the divine order was ever introduced until the church set out upon the reckless career of adopting practices in religion at the mere dictate of human wisdom. The great danger at this point was anticipated by divine wisdom, and many solemn warnings were placed on record against it.*

IV. FROM THE VERY EARLIEST INTRODUCTION OF THIS PRACTICE, IT EXCITED STRENUOUS AND PROLONGED OPPOSITION.

This fact is abundantly set forth in Bingham's Antiquities, in many of the Church Histories, and in the standard encyclopedias. Their testimony, as it bears upon different phases of the subject, will be cited in its proper place.

V. THE NEW TESTAMENT TERMS WHICH DESCRIBE AND ENJOIN THE ELEMENT OF MUSIC IN CHRISTIAN WORSHIP.

Confining our statement to the terms which specifically indicate music, these are the verbs *ado* (ᾄδω),

---

*See particularly the following passages: 1 Cor. 1: 20-29; 4: 6; 2 John 9; Rev. 22: 18, 19, *et al.*

humneo (ὑμνέω), and psallo (ψάλλω), and their cognate nouns ode (ᾠδή), hymnos (ὕμνος), and psalmos (ψαλμός). There has never been any controversy over the kind of music, in general, indicated by the first two of these verbs and their nouns, nor, indeed, has there been any, until recent years, over the meaning of psallo (ψάλλω) and its noun; but, all other efforts failing to discover a basis of divine authority for instrumental music in Christian worship, some of its advocates in modern times have alleged, as a *dernier ressort,* that the term psallo (ψάλλω), as used in the New Testament, involves the use of an instrumental accompaniment, and that, therefore, the practice rests upon divine authority. The argument based upon this allegation is not only sometimes made with apparent fairness and with some degree of force, but it often appears plausible and in some instances conclusive. It is, therefore, worthy of careful examination and consideration. Moreover, the bare fact that the classical meaning of psallo (ψάλλω), at some periods of its history, involves instrumental music, together with the widespread tendency to a confusion of the classical with the New Testament meaning, furnishes an additional reason for meeting such apologists on their own chosen ground.

On this account, it is now proposed to subject this claim and the reasoning based on it, to a fair and legitimate, but rigid and crucial test by a direct appeal to the facts of philology and of history. It is the purpose to present a careful induction of all the facts in the case which modern scholarship has brought to light, and to weigh impartially the evidence on both sides of the question. In the whole field of argumentation covered by the various and multifarious discussions of this question for more than a quarter of a century, nothing has appeared which, in the present writer's judgment, contains a more deceptive and misleading fallacy than that which lurks in the argument based on this modern claim concerning the term *psallo* (ψάλλω), and it is now proposed to present, from different fields of evidence, an array of facts which, it is devoutly believed, will thoroughly and successfully expose the fallacy to all unprejudiced minds competent to judge of such matters. While it is the aim to conduct the investigation, in the main, in the form of an inquiry into the history and meaning of *psallo* (ψάλλω), other features of the controversy will be duly considered, and it is confidently believed that the induction of testimony presented in this volume, from numerous and various sources, is sufficiently ample and strong to satisfy the most rigid demands of all candid, thoughtful, and unbiased minds. In the meantime, my readers are respectfully invited to examine the evidence for themselves, and to render their own verdict in the case.

CHAPTER II.

Psallo as Defined by the Lexicons.

That we may have a clear anu comprehensive view of the history and meaning of this famous word, we now appeal to that important and most interesting class of authorities embraced in the broad field of Greek lexicography; and that our conclusions may rest upon a solid basis of fact, we appeal to all the authorities occupying this field as far as we have been able, by a diligent and prolonged search, to gain access to them. They are summoned from all ranks regardless of their theological training and affiliation. In fact, in order that our induction of testimony from this source may be impartial and complete, we shall call on some witnesses from this class to testify who do not occupy a place in the highest rank as authorities. To speak plainly, a few of them are not standard authorities at all. They are quoted in this work, not because their testimony either strengthens or in any way materially affects the case one way or the other, but simply because they are relied on and sometimes appealed to in discussions of the question by persons of respectable standing and ability, and it is earnestly desired in the prosecution of the present inquiry, to leave no stone unturned in the search for facts.

6

But while it is thought best, for the reason stated, to include such witnesses in the present work, the reader will find that, in addition to these, the list contains, also, by the unanimous consent of scholars, the very highest authorities in existence. The author has spared no pains in the search for authorities in this field; and, so far as lexical authority is concerned, it is confidently believed that the list herewith presented will give the reader access to what may be justly regarded as the voice of scholarship in the English-speaking world of to-day. Truth is the exclusive object of our search, and the testimony of witnesses is cheerfully welcomed and impartially considered, regardless of the side on which its weight may seem to fall.

A careful survey of the field of evidence furnished by lexicographers of every grade has led the author to the decided conviction that there is not a solitary fact in all history touching the meaning of *psallo* which, considered in the light of its proper connection and bearing, can be legitimately used to sustain the practice of instrumental music in the worship of God under Christ. On the contrary, the testimony of the very lexicons sometimes offered to sustain the practice only confirms, when properly examined and weighed, the position defended in this volume, namely, that in the evolution of the Greek language during the course of centuries, the term underwent several changes and modifications. Moreover, we shall see that this view of the question is confirmed by the very highest lexical authorities in existence to-day.

There is a right way, and there is a wrong way to use lexicons; and it is not strange that young minds, uninformed concerning the evolution of words in the history of a language, should be misled by, and hence misapply, a definition which they find in a lexicon. It would be an easy matter for a beginner in the study of the English language to make this mistake in the use of English dictionaries. Lexicons are neither commentaries nor histories, and yet it is their business to furnish examples of the varied use and application of words, and such examples become at once an index to the history of the words thus defined. This shows that, in unskillful hands, a lexicon may be so used as to appear to disprove what it really proves, and, *vice versa,* to prove what it really disproves. Hence, next to the value of a lexicon itself, is the importance of knowing how to use it. Later on we shall have further use for what these distinguished authorities in the field of lexicography have to say, but, first of all, the reader's attention is invited to their definitions which have been copied with special care for this work, and in nearly every instance they have been copied under the direct supervision of the author himself. The quotations as here given can, therefore, be relied on as strictly correct. The aim in this chapter is simply to present a collation of the definitions as given by the lexicons, and no stress is laid upon the mere order in which they are quoted. We shall now hear, in their own words, these distinguished witnesses on the meaning of *psallo*.

I. Liddell and Scott: "ψάλλω [*psallo*], *to touch sharply, to pluck, pull, twitch, to pluck* the hair, of the bowstring, *to twang* it; *to send* a shaft *twanging* from the bow; so, σχοῖνος μιλτοφυρὴς ψαλλομένη a carpenter's red line, which *is twitched* and then suddenly let go, so as to leave a mark. II. mostly of the string of musical instruments, *to play* a stringed instrument *with the fingers,* and not with the plectron. 2. later, *to sing to a harp;* Lxx. (Ps. 7:17; 9:11; al.), Eph. 5:19; 1 Cor. 14:15. 3. *to be struck* or *played; to be played to on the harp.*"

The noun *psalmos* (ψαλμός): "*a touching sharply, a pulling, twitching* or *twanging* with the fingers. II. mostly of musical strings. 2. *the sound of the cithara* or *harp.* 3. later, *a song sung to the harp, a psalm,* Lxx., N. T."

II. Robinson: "ψάλλω [*psallo*], *to touch, to twitch, to pluck,* e. g. the hair or beard; also a string, *to twang,* e. g. the string of a bow; especially of a stringed instrument of music, *to touch* or *strike the chords.* Hence oftenest absolutely ψάλλειν, *to touch the lyre* or other stringed instrument, *to strike up, to play.* In Septuagint and New Testament *to sing, to chant,* properly as accompanying stringed instruments."

In the noun form, *psalmos* (ψαλμός): "*a touching, twang,* e. g. of a bowstring; of stringed instruments,

9

a playing, music; tone, melody, measure, as played.
In later usage, *song,* properly as accompanying
stringed instruments. 1. *a psalm, a song,* in praise
of God; 1 Cor. 14: 26; Eph. 5: 19; Col. 3: 16. 2.
specifically Plural *the Psalms,* the book of Psalms.''

III. PICKERING: ''ψάλλω [*psallo*], to touch gently;
to touch or play on a stringed instrument; to cause
to vibrate; to play; to celebrate with hymns; to pull
or pluck, *as the hair.*''

The noun, *psalmos* (ψαλμός): ''the twang of a bowstring; striking the chords of a musical instrument;
playing and singing to the psaltery; a psalm, an ode,
a hymn.''

IV. GROVES: *''ψάλλω [psallo], to touch, strike
softly; to play on the harp; to sing to the harp; to
praise, celebrate.''*

''ψαλμός [psalmos], a singing to or *playing on the
harp; the sound of a stringed instrument; a psalm,
hymn.''*

V. DONNEGAN: ''ψάλλω [*psallo*], to touch and cause
to move *or* cause vibration; to touch, *as the string
of a bow, and thus,* discharge an arrow, *or the strings
of a musical instrument,* and play; (*with* κιθάραν *understood*) to play on the harp (*when the* 'plectrum'
is used, the term is κρέκω)—to scrape; to pull *or* pluck,
as the hair.''

''ψαλμος [psalmos], properly, the act of touching
and putting in motion; the act of touching the string
of a bow, and letting fly an arrow; *also,* the touching
of the chords of a musical instrument, a playing on

10

a harp, *or* similar instrument (*see* ψάλλω)—an air played on a harp, *Pindar, also by later writers,* a hymn, *or* ode sung accompanied by a harp."

VI. Parkhurst: "ψάλλω [psallo], 1. *To touch, touch lightly,* or perhaps *to cause to quaver by touching.* 2. *To touch the strings* of a musical instrument with the finger or plectrum, and so *cause* them *to sound* or *quaver.* So musicians who play upon an instrument are said χορδὰς ψάλλειν, *to touch the strings,* or simply ψάλλειν. And because *stringed* instruments were commonly used both by Believers and Heathen in *singing praises* to their respective Gods, hence 3. *To sing, sing praises* or *psalms to God,* whether with or without instruments. Rom. 15: 9; 1 Cor. 14: 15; Eph. 5: 19; Jas. 5: 13.

"ψαλμός [*psalmos*], 1. *A touching* or *playing upon a musical instrument.* 2. *A psalm, a sacred song* or *poem,* properly such an one as is sung to *stringed instruments.* See Luke 20: 42; 1 Cor. 14: 26."

VII. Dunbar: "ψάλλω [*psallo*], to touch gently; to touch *or* play on a stringed instrument; to sing; to celebrate with hymns."

"ψαλμός [*psalmos*], the twang of a bowstring; a playing on a stringed instrument, singing to the psaltery; a psalm; a song."

VIII. Bagster: "ψάλλω [*psallo*], *to move by a touch, to twitch; to touch, strike* the strings or chords of an instrument; absolutely *to play on a stringed instrument; to sing to music;* in New Testament *to*

11

sing praises, Rom. 15: 9; 1 Cor. 14: 15; Eph. 5: 19; Jas. 5: 13.''

''ψαλμός [*psalmos*], *impulse, touch,* of the chords of a stringed instrument; in New Testament *a sacred song, psalm,* 1 Cor. 14: 26; Eph. 5: 19, *et al.*''

IX. M. WRIGHT: ''ψάλλω [*psallo*], I cause vibration, touch; discharge an arrow; scrape; pluck.''

''ψαλμός [*psalmos*], playing on a harp; air played on a harp, hymn; twang of a string.''

X. W. GREENFIELD: ''ψάλλω [*psallo*], to touch, strike *the strings or chords of an instrument;* hence absolutely to touch or strike the chords, play on a stringed instrument, namely, *as an accompaniment tc the voice;* by implication to sing, and *with a dative of person,* to sing in honor or praise of, sing praises to, celebrate in song or psalm, Rom. 15: 9; 1 Cor. 14: 15; Eph. 5: 19; Jas. 5: 13.''

''ψαλμός [*psalmos*], impulse, touch, *of the chords of a stringed instrument;* an ode, song; a sacred song, psalm, 1 Cor. 14: 26; Eph. 5: 19.''

XI. YONGE—*English-Greek Lexicon:* ''To play, νηπιαχεύω; ἀθύρω; παίζω. *To play on an instrument,* see above; also μέλπομαι; κρέκω; ψάλλω (only of playing on stringed instruments).''

XII. CONTOPOULOS' *New Greek-English and English-Greek:* ''ψάλλω [*psallo*], v. a. v. n. to sing, to celebrate; (μεταφ.) τόυ τἄψαλα, I gave him a good lecture.'' —''ψαλμῳδός, a psalmist, a singer of psalms, a bard, a minstrel.''

XIII. EDWARD MALTBY'S GREEK GRADUS: "ψάλλω (*psallo*) to strike gently, 2. to pull *the string of a bow*, or *of a harp*. 3. to praise."

XIV. HAMILTON: "ψάλλω [*psallo*], to touch, pull, pluck, cause to vibrate, play on a stringed instrument, sing."

"ψαλμός [*psalmos*], playing on a harp, twang of a string, strain of music, hymn, song."

XV. THAYER: "ψάλλω [*psallo*], a. *to pluck off, pull out:* ἔθειραν, the hair. b. *to cause to vibrate by touching, to twang:* specifically *to touch* or *strike the chord, to twang the strings* of a musical instrument so that they gently vibrate; and absolutely *to play on a stringed instrument, to play the harp,* etc.; Septuagint for *niggēn* and much oftener for *zimmēr; to sing to the music of the harp;* in the New Testament *to sing a hymn, to celebrate the praises of God in song,* Jas. 5: 13; in honor of God, Eph. 5: 19; Rom. 15: 9; ψαλῶ τῷ πνεύματι, ψαλῶ δὲ καὶ τῷ νοΐ, 'I will sing God's praises indeed with my whole soul stirred and borne away by the Holy Spirit, but I will also follow reason as my guide, so that what I sing may be understood alike by myself and by the listeners,' 1 Cor. 14: 15."

"ψαλμός [psalmos], *a striking, twanging;* specifically *a striking the chords* of a musical instrument; hence *a pious song, a psalm* (Septuagint chiefly for *mizmōr*), Eph. 5: 19; Col. 3: 16; the phrase ἔχειν ψαλμόν is used of one who has it in his heart to sing or recite a song of the sort, 1 Cor. 14: 26; one of the songs of the book of the Old Testament which is entitled ψαλμοί, Acts 13: 23.''

XVI. SOPHOCLES: ''ψάλλω [psallo], to chant, sing religious hymns. Sept. Judic. 5: 3. Paul. 1 Cor. 14: 15. Jacob. 5: 13.''

''ψαλμός [psalmos], psalm.''

XVII. THOMAS SHELDON GREEN: ''Ψάλλω [psallo] to move by a touch, to twitch; to touch, strike *the strings or chords of an instrument;* absolutely to play on a stringed instrument; to sing to music; *in New Testament,* to sing praises, Rom. 15: 9; 1 Cor. 14: 15; Eph. 5: 19; Jas. 5: 13: *whence*

''Ψαλμός, impulse, touch, *of the chords of a stringed instrument; in New Testament,* a sacred song, psalm, 1 Cor. 14: 26; Eph. 5: 19, et al.''

We now have before us the definitions of seventeen Greek-English Lexicons. For the sake of avoiding a circumlocution in the translation of definitions, we have omitted from the list all of the lexicons whose definitions are in Latin or any other language than English. However, a faithful translation of all of these would yield no substantial variation in meaning from those given by the Greek-English Lexicons. Hence, in the definitions already presented, we have substantially the combined testimony of all extant Greek lexicography on the meaning of *psallo.*

One of the first things likely to strike the reader is the great number and variety of meanings which, as now seen in the lexicons, the word *psallo* has borne at one time or another during its history. Further-

14

more, these meanings, as will be seen, are not only diverse one from another, but some of them seem, at first sight, to be wholly foreign to each other. However, we shall find, upon close examination, that they all carry with them, either literally or figuratively, *the one original and unvarying idea denoted by the word.* Let these facts all be noted with care, for we shall have use for them later on in our investigation.

The reader will also please note the fact that, in the midst of this variety of meanings, the learned authorities quoted testify, with great unanimity and clearness, that *psallo,* at some time during its history, signified touching the chords of a musical instrument, and hence that it meant to make instrumental music. It is here frankly conceded that the word once had this meaning, and it is the author's wish that this fact shall have all the weight to which it is entitled in the present inquiry. Truth has nothing to fear either from a candid admission of facts, or from the most searching and rigid investigation, and its friends and advocates should be willing at all times to admit a fact, when it is seen to be a fact. These numerous and various definitions will be clearly and fully accounted for in due time, and the reader will then be prepared to see how they all combine to support the position contended for in the present volume. A final verdict on the main question at issue should be withheld till all the facts are heard from.

PSALLO AS DEFINED BY THE LEXICONS.

In the meantime, as an aid to a proper appreciation of the argument from the lexicons, we present here a summary of their definitions:

1. *Radical meaning*, TO TOUCH, regardless of the particular object touched, the latter not inhering in the word.

2. *Meanings as applied in Greek literature:*

(1) To pluck the hair.

(2) To twang the bowstring.

(3) To twitch a carpenter's line.

(4) To touch the chords of a musical instrument, that is, to make instrumental music.

(5) To touch the chords of the human heart, that is, to sing, to celebrate with hymns of praise.

3. Thus, according to the lexicons, here are five separate and distinct meanings of *psallo* (ψάλλω) growing out of the original idea, all of which it has borne at one time or another during the progress of the centuries. Now, in view of these facts, what shall we say is the meaning of this word? Out of five well-defined and distinct meanings, shall we select one of them, and then affirm, regardless of the time when used, or any other circumstance, that *this* is the meaning of the word? If so, which one of the five meanings shall it be, and why? As we have them here numbered, shall it be the first one? If so, why so? If not, why not? According to the highest standard authorities, the word at one time meant "*to pluck the hair.*" Now, when Christians assemble to worship God, may they proceed, Nehemiah-like (Neh.

13: 25), "to pluck off their hair" as a part of that worship? If not, why not? Does the reader say that such an act in the worship of God would be silly? We reply that it would, indeed, be silly, and sinful, too, for that matter, but certainly not because that was not a meaning of *psallo*. Such worshipers could promptly defend themselves by appealing both to the Greek lexicons and to the Bible. They could show from standard Greek lexicons that "*psallo*" had that meaning, and that the New Testament authorizes them, if we may accept a coined word, to "*psallo*."

The same course could be pursued with reference to the second and third meanings, which are "to twang the bowstring" and "to twitch a carpenter's line." Both of these were meanings of "psallo" vouched for by lexicons of the highest authority. May we, therefore, contend for *twanging the bowstring* and *twitching the carpenter's line* IN THE WORSHIP OF GOD? If not, why not? If it be replied that these are meanings which the word had before the New Testament period, but that in the New Testament it has no such meaning, then we reply by admitting the fact, and making the point that this is precisely what is true of the fourth meaning also. This fact will abundantly appear as our investigation proceeds.

In the meantime, we now see the necessity for wise discrimination in the use of lexicons, and that it does not follow, because a given definition of a word appears in a lexicon, that therefore the word always had, and still has, that meaning.

CHAPTER III.

The Periods of the Greek Language.

Both the time when, and the place where, a given Greek word had a given meaning, constitute such an important factor in the making of Greek lexicons, that Liddell and Scott found it necessary to place Demosthenes and Aristotle, although both of these illustrious men were born the same year and both died the same year, in different epochs. Of course the same formative and revolutionary influences, which produced such an effect on the language of strictly contemporaneous speakers and writers, would operate with still greater effect through the long process of centuries.

In the Preface to their Greek lexicon, Liddell and Scott say:

The date of each author's "floruit" is added in the margin; and, by comparing this with the short summary of the chief Epochs of Greek literature prefixed to the Catalogue, it will be easy to determine the time of a word's first use, and of its subsequent changes of signification. It will be understood, however, that the age of a word does not wholly depend on that of its Author. For, first, many Greek books have been lost; secondly, a word of Attic stamp, first occurring in Lucian, Alciphron,

18

or later imitators of Attic Greek, may be considered as virtually older than those found in the vernacular writers of the Alexandrian age. Further, the language changed differently in different places at the same time; as in the cases of Demosthenes and Aristotle, whom we have been compelled to place in different Epochs. And even at the same place, as at Athens, there were naturally two parties, one clinging to old usages, the other fond of what was new. The Greek of Thucydides and Lysias may be compared in illustration of this remark.—*Page* VI.

Referring to the radical changes and modifications of the Greek language in the different epochs of its history, Sophocles, in the Introduction to his great lexicon, says:

In the second century of our era the language had deviated perceptibly from the ancient standard. Old words and expressions had disappeared, and new ones succeeded them. In addition to this, new meanings were put upon old words. The syntax, moreover, was undergoing some changes. Further, Latinisms and other foreign idioms were continually creeping into the language of common life. The purists of the day made an effort to check this tendency, but they were steadily opposed by usage, and not infrequently by good sense.—*Page* 6.

Then, on page 8, the same author says:

The writers of the New Testament, and of the Apocrypha, strictly so called, were Hellenists. They used the Common Dialect as spoken by Jews of limited education. And as there was a great gulf between the doctrines propagated by the Apostles and the religion of the Greeks, these writers were sometimes obliged to give new meanings to old words and expressions.

Edwin Hatch, in "Essays in Biblical Greek," says:

The differences between the language of Athens in the fourth century before Christ and the language of the New Testament may be roughly described as differences of time and differences of country. I. Many differences were the natural result of the lapse of time. For Greek was a living language, and a living language is always in movement. It was kept in motion partly by causes external to itself and partly by the causes which are always at work in the speech of all civilized races.—*Page* 3.

Explaining his purpose in giving frequently in his New Testament lexicon an exposition of classic usage, Thayer says:

The frequent references in the discussion of synonymous terms, to the distinctions holding in classic usage (as they are laid down by Schmidt in his voluminous work) must not be regarded as designed to modify the definitions given in the several articles. On the contrary, the exposition of classic usage is often intended merely to serve as a standard of comparison by which the direction and degree of a word's change in meaning can be measured. When so employed, the information given will often start suggestions alike interesting and instructive.—*Preface to Thayer's Lexicon*, p. VII.

I have no wish to multiply authorities beyond the legitimate demands of the case, but cannot resist giving the reader the benefit, in this connection, of the following significant quotation from the scholarly Preface to Dr. Robinson's lexicon. A careful study of this learned author's Preface not only throws light on the purpose of lexicons in general, but it shows the minute and extended labor which he bestowed upon his own lexicon. Discussing the different Epochs of the Greek language and the various changes and modifications to which it was subject, Dr. Robinson says:

A full and scientific lexicon of any language embraces a wide field of inquiry. The scholar who would pursue the study of a language critically and philosophically, does not rest until he has traced each word to its origin; investigated its primitive form and signification; noted the various forms and senses in which it has been current in the different epochs and dialects of the language, and the manner and order in which all these are deduced from the primitive one and from each other; and last, though not least, has observed the relations in which it stands to other words, in constructions and phrases, and the various modifications which it has undergone in these respects.—*Page* IV.

Finally, on page V., commenting on these general linguistic characteristics as exhibited in the Greek language in particular, the same author says:

In respect to the Greek, it should be borne in mind that there are three great epochs which mark the

21

progress of the language; through all or some of which, the different meanings and uses of a word can be traced with more or less distinctness. These are the youth, in the heroic or epic poems of Homer and Hesiod, with which may be joined the Ionic prose of Herodotus; its prime, in the palmy days of Attic elegance and purity, as exhibited in the great tragedians, and in the prose of Thucydides, Xenophon, Plato; and its decline, after the Macedonian conquest, and still later under the Roman dominion. In this latter period, the breaking up of the various independent states, the mingling together in armies of soldiers enlisted from every quarter, and the founding of colonies and large cities peopled with inhabitants from every part of Greece and also from foreign lands, could not fail to produce great changes in the languages of different communities; which, by natural consequence, would speedily be reflected in the language of books. Thus was formed the later Greek idiom (ἡ κοινὴ διάλεκτος), which everywhere superseded the pure Attic; and of which Aristotle, Polybius, Diodorus, Plutarch, Ælian, and other later writers are the representatives.

Here is the combined testimony of the distinguished scholars who occupy the highest place as lexicographers in the estimation of present-day scholarship, all to the effect that *when* and *where* a word was used, often has much to do with its meaning. Accordingly, in the study of any Greek word, it is of the greatest importance to keep constantly in mind what these masters of the classics are pleased to term the different periods of the language.

22

These, as given by Sophocles in his lexicon, are as follows:

I. The Mythical Period, the time prior to Homer.

II. The Ionic Period, from Homer to B.C. 500.

III. The Attic Period, from B.C. 500 to B.C. 283.

IV. The Alexandrian Period, from B.C. 283 to B.C. 146.

V. The Roman Period, from B.C. 146 to A.D. 330.

VI. The Byzantine Period, from A.D. 330 to A.D. 1453.

Other scholars, notably Liddell and Scott, vary slightly from Sophocles both as to number and exact time of the periods, but they are all in substantial agreement on all essential matters and reach, practically, the same conclusion. There is not a dissenting voice among them touching the existence of such well-defined periods and the necessity for recognizing them in an attempt to arrive at the true meaning and history of a word. We are not to suppose that attention to these periods or epochs in the evolution of a language will disclose sudden changes in the meaning of words. Long periods sometimes elapse before a word is found to have undergone a complete change in meaning. On this point, Sophocles deposes as follows:

Changes in a language are not instantaneous, but come on by insensible gradations, and therefore it is impossible to fix the precise time of transition from one stage to another. Thus, although the period of the highest development of the language of

Athens coincides with the Persian, Peloponnesian, and Macedonian troubles, we are not to infer that it began on the day after the burning of Sardis and ended with the death of Alexander.—*Introduction to Lexicon,* p. 11.

It must now be evident to the thoughtful reader that, when the lexicons attach a given meaning to a word, we should still inquire, *When did the word have that meaning? or, Did the word have that meaning at one time or place, and then cease to have it at another time or place?* And hence, any argument based on our term *psallo* (ψάλλω) which does not take account of all these facts and considerations is unsound and misleading.

Now, it is a significant fact that all the authors quoted by the lexicons to sustain the assumption that instrumental music is involved in this word, belong, with three exceptions, to periods of the Greek language antedating the New Testament period; and the exceptions, as we shall see later on in our investigation, can be accounted for on theological grounds. Including all the authors quoted by all the lexicons to which we have been able to find access, there are Euripides, Plato, Aristotle, Athenæus, Herodotus, Ion Chius, Aristophanes, Lucian, Macho, the Septuagint, Dionysius of Halicarnassus, the New Testament, Josephus, and Plutarch. Here are fourteen authorities quoted by the various lexicons, and the entire list, with three exceptions, as previously stated, are embraced in the period from 450 years

24

B.C. to 30 years B.C. This fact speaks loudly, and speaks with significance, provided we can properly account for the exceptions. They shall receive due attention later on in the investigation.

CHAPTER IV.

Change of Meaning in the History of Words.

We are now prepared for the testimony of specialists in the department of philology, and to witness an exemplification of the principles advanced in the preceding chapters.

In the whole realm of philology, there is, perhaps, no fact more evident than the change of meaning incident to words in a living language. Just as the customs, habits, occupations, and usages of a people are subject to change under the influence of changing conditions and circumstances, so the language of a people, for similar reasons, is subject to change. In proof of this, and as a final preparation for the consideration of specific examples, we now introduce the testimony of distinguished philologists who have made the study of language a specialty, and whose word, therefore, is the highest authority to which we can appeal in this department. It is immaterial whether the authorities quoted on this point be of recent or earlier date, the only essential consideration being that their testimony is reliable concerning the character and genius of language in general.

1. We will first hear Professor Max Müller, the brilliant lecturer on ''The Science of Language'' at

the Royal Institution of Great Britain in 1861, who said:

Every part of nature, whether mineral, plant, or animal, is the same in kind from the beginning to the end of its existence, whereas few languages could be recognized as the same after the lapse of but a thousand years. The language of Alfred is so different from the English of the present day that we have to study it in the same manner as we study Greek and Latin. We can read Milton and Bacon, Shakespeare and Hooker; we can make out Wycliff and Chaucer; but when we come to the English of the thirteenth century, we can but guess its meaning.—*Science of Language,* p. 34.

The same eminent authority makes the following statement:

The language of the Authorized Version of the Bible, though perfectly intelligible, is no longer the spoken language of England. In Booker's Scripture and Prayer-book Glossary the number of words or senses of words which have become obsolete since 1611, amount to 388, or nearly one-fifteenth part of the whole number of words used in the Bible.—*Ibid.* p. 35.

This is not only strong testimony, but it gives no uncertain sound on the special point now before us, namely, that change of meaning in words is so common to all living languages that, on an average, about one word out of every fifteen in the common version of the Bible underwent a complete change in meaning in the course of two hundred and fifty years.

2. Professor A. H. Sayce, who occupies the Chair of Comparative Philology in the University of Oxford, and who is the author of several interesting works on the higher criticism of the Bible, says:

Language and languages are in a constant state of change: nowhere, indeed, can the maxim of Heraclitus, πάντα 'ρεῖ, be better illustrated. This perpetual flux and change is necessitated by the very fact that language is a product and creation of the human mind. Thought is ever shifting, moving, developing, and so, too, is the language in which it seeks to embody itself.—*Introduction to the Science of Language,* Vol. I., p. 166.

3. In the interesting and valuable "Lectures on the English Language" by George P. Marsh, we find this significant testimony:

The changes of signification which words undergo in all languages, from mere exhaustion by use, is a far more extensive and important subject. "Names and words," says Robertson, "soon lose their meaning. In the process of years and centuries, the meaning dies off them like the sunlight from the hills. The hills are there, the color is gone."—P. 255.

4. Benjamin W. Dwight, another master of language and literature, testifies in the following interesting manner:

Words pine away and die as truly as men themselves and books. Many whole languages have disappeared in other days, as in every language many words are perpetually losing their vitality like Autumn leaves that have fulfilled their use, and, when their "occupation is gone," drop useless to the ground themselves.—*Modern Philology, Second Series*, p. 287.

5. To the same effect, Archbishop Trench, the renowned author of the "Study of Words," adds the following testimony:

The rise and fall of words, the honor which in tract of time they exchanged for dishonor, and the dishonor for honor—all which in my last lecture I contemplated mainly from an ethical point of view—is in a merely historic aspect less remarkable. Very curious is it to watch the varying fortune of words—the extent to which it has fared with them as with persons and families; some having improved their position in the world, and attained to far higher dignity than seemed destined for them at the beginning, while others in a manner quite as notable have lost caste, have descended from their high estate to common and even ignoble uses. Titles of dignity and honor have naturally a peculiar liability to be some lifted up, and some cast down. Of words which have risen in the world, the French "maréchal" affords us an excellent example. "Maréchal," as Howell has said, "at first was the name of a smith-farrier, or one that dressed horses"—which indeed it is still—"but it climbed by degrees to that height that the chiefest commanders of the gendarmery are come to be called marshals." But if this has risen, our "alderman" has fallen. Whatever the civic dignity of an alderman may now be, still it must be owned that the word has lost much since the time that the "alderman" was only second in rank and position to the king.—*Study of Words*, pp. 208, 209.

6. The scholarly John Peile, who was one time teacher of Sanskrit in the University of Cambridge, the author of a valuable Introduction to Greek and Latin Etymology, and of a more recent work on Philology, has given to the public, as a part of the fruit of his varied learning and researches, much valuable information on our theme. He devotes one chapter to "The Constant Change in Language;" and, after quoting a passage from Shakespeare's Macbeth, and showing how radically some of its words have changed in meaning, he says:

Thus we have examined one passage, and have found in its four lines seven words which are either not used now at all, or are used in a different sense. . . . We must admit then that the English of to-day differs much from Shakespeare's English in the meaning of its words.—*Philology*, pp. 10, 11.

7. The eminent logician, John Stuart Mill, says:

These and similar instances in which the original signification of a term is totally lost—another and an entirely distinct meaning being first engrafted upon the former, and finally substituted for it—afford examples of the double movement which is always taking place in language: the counter-movements, one of Generalization, by which words are perpetually losing portions of their connotation and becoming of less meaning and more general acceptation; the other Specialization, by which other, or even

30

these same words, are continually taking on fresh connotation; acquiring additional meaning by being restricted in their employment to a part only of the occasions on which they might properly be used before.—*System of Logic*, p. 416.

8. Finally, from the eloquent Walter Scott we have the following significant deliverance:

Language is unstable, liable to change and corruption. Words are constantly losing their primitive meaning, and by the refining and discriminating processes by which they multiply themselves, are constantly losing their original significance and distinctness. The English word "form" has repeated itself in forty different derivatives.—*Messiahship, or Great Demonstration,* p. 10.

From such testimonies, taken directly from the writings of some of the world's most distinguished linguists and philologists, the conclusion follows, with overwhelming force, that the meaning of a word in a given language at one time may not be its meaning at another time. It is a fact, however, that concrete examples are worth more to the average mind, in an investigation like this, than abstract testimonies taken even from the world's greatest scholars. Hence, it is my purpose to present now, from our own language, a number of examples illustrating the theory of constant change in the meaning of words in all living languages which has been submitted and argued at some length in the foregoing pages. For this purpose, I have selected a list of English words whose meaning to-day was never even thought of in the earlier periods of the language, and whose meaning then is now obsolete. Let the reader carefully study the examples here submitted.

1. The word *carp*. In the English of to-day, this word means "to find fault; to cavil; to censure;" and no writer or speaker of good English would use it now in any other sense; but in Chaucer's time— that is, in the latter half of the fourteenth century, it meant simply "to converse," or to engage in conversation. This sense is now entirely lost, and if any one should attempt to use the word thus to-day, he would not be understood. The word has undergone a complete change in meaning, and retains nothing in common with what it once was, except the bare idea of *speech.*

2. The word *resent*. This word vividly illustrates the point before us. According to its Latin etymology, it literally means to exercise one's feelings in return for some kindly deed done by another; in other words, to express kindly feelings for favors received. Hence, when it first made its appearance in the history of the English language, it bore, in large measure, the meaning now attached to the word *"reciprocate,"* and it was good English in the seventeenth century, as Archbishop Trench observes, to speak of "an affectionate 'resentment' of our obligations to God. But," continues the same author, "the memory of benefits fades from us so much more quickly than that of injuries; we remember and re-

volve in our minds so much more predominantly the wrongs, real or imaginary, men have done us, than the favors we owe them, that 'resentment' has come in our modern English to be confined exclusively to that deep reflective displeasure which men entertain against those that have done, or whom they fancy to have done, them a wrong." And so the only meaning which the word has to-day is "to be indignant at, to express or exhibit displeasure or indignation at." If an Englishman had used it in this latter sense two hundred and fifty years ago, he would have been unintelligible; and it is equally true that if it were used to-day in the sense it bore then, it would be unintelligible.

3. The word *timeserver*. According to its unvarying meaning in present-day English, the very mention of this word suggests a person whose conduct is contemptible. Webster defines it: "One who adapts his opinions and manners to the times; one who obsequiously complies with the ruling power." And yet two hundred and fifty years ago it indicated one whose conduct was honorable, meaning nothing more than one "serving the time."

4. The word *candidate*. This familiar word is derived from a Latin word meaning *white,* and in the mouth of either Livy or Cicero a person running for public office was called a "candidate" (*candidatus*), not because the word denotes any such fact, but from the circumstance that such persons, according to Roman custom, were clothed in *white.* But to-day

this idea is so completely gone from the word that it is never suggested by the popular use of the term candidate, which, regardless of the garment worn, is simply "one who offers himself, or is put forward by others, as a suitable person or an aspirant or contestant for an office, privilege, or honor; as, a candidate for the office of governor; a candidate for holy orders; a candidate for scholastic honors."— *Webster*. In popular usage to-day the average person, when speaking of a candidate for office, never thinks of the white toga worn by the ancient Romans. The word no longer has this meaning, and but few persons, comparatively, know that it ever had such a meaning.

5. The word *animosity*. In the fifteenth century this word simply meant "mere spiritedness or courage," and this meaning is true to the Latin origin of the term. It is from a word which denotes the soul, spirit, or mind, and in the verb form, to breathe; hence, it was natural that its first meaning should be "spiritedness or courage," a meaning still preserved in the kindred words "animate" and "animated;" but this meaning is now entirely gone from the word animosity, whose only meaning is: "Violent hatred leading to active opposition; active enmity; energetic dislike."

6. The word *prevent*. Just as we have seen in some other examples, so in "prevent" the idea in its Latin original prevailed for a time. It is made up of a preposition meaning "before," and a verb mean-

ing "to go;" hence, three hundred years ago it meant: "To go before; to precede; hence to go before as a guide; to direct;" and in the Book of Common Prayer in the seventeenth century we find this petition to the Lord: "We pray Thee that thy grace may always *prevent* and follow us." Of course this usage of the word would be wholly out of place and misleading to-day; yet, in the Common Version of the English Bible, sometimes called the Authorized or King James Version, which was made in A.D. 1611, it is used in precisely this sense, which, with similar examples and facts, constituted one of the reasons for a Revision of the English of that version. It is used in that version in the sense in question in the following passages: "But unto thee have I cried, O Lord; and in the morning shall my prayer prevent thee," Psa. 88: 13. "I prevented the dawning of the morning, and cried," Psa. 119: 147. "Mine eyes prevent the night watches, that I might meditate in thy word," Psa. 119: 148. "And when he was come into the house, Jesus prevented him, saying," etc., Matt. 17: 25. "We which are alive and remain unto the coming of the Lord shall not prevent them which are asleep." 1 Thess. 4: 15.

From the use of the word in these passages, the reader can easily see that some such term as "anticipate," "precede," or "go before" must be substituted for "prevent" in order to make good sense, because the latter, in present-day English, always means "to intercept; to hinder; to frustrate; to stop;

35

to thwart." Its ancient literal meaning, which it retained for several centuries, has wholly disappeared, so that in the sense of "to go before" it is now never used, but invariably conveys the idea of *hindering.*

7. The word *lewd.* Unless my readers have given special attention to the history. of this word, they will no doubt be surprised to hear that it first meant the *common people* in distinction from the *clergy.* Remotely connected with the Greek word *laos* (λαός) meaning people, it made its way through Old English and Anglo-Saxon as the equivalent of *laical,* that is, "belonging to the laity" in distinction from the clergy. But, as the clergy were ordinarily distinguished from the common people by superior learning, so the first meaning of "lewd" was: "Not clerical; laic; laical; hence, unlearned; simple." In this sense, it was used by Chaucer in the couplet:

> For if a priest be foul, on whom we trust,
> No wonder is a lewd man to rust.

But, what a broad chasm between its meaning then, and its meaning now! It now means: "Given to the promiscuous indulgence of lust; dissolute, lustful; libidinous;" or, "suiting, or proceeding from, lustfulness; involving unlawful sexual desire; as, lewd thoughts, conduct, or language;" and in this sense it is universally used to-day. But it did not cross this chasm at one bound. Three hundred years ago, before it had acquired any of the meaning which it

36

now has, it lingered for a time with the meaning: "Belonging to the lower classes, or the rabble; idle and lawless; bad; vicious;" and it found its way into the Authorized Version of the Bible with this meaning in Acts 17:5—"But the Jews which believed not, moved with envy, took unto them certain lewd fellows of the baser sort," etc. Thus, the word was passing through a process of continuous change before it reached the meaning which clings to it to-day.

8. The word *idiot*. This word furnishes a fine illustration of our principle. It is really a Greek word (ἰδιώτης, from ἴδιος, one's own, private), and originally meant, "one in a private station, opposed to one holding public office, or taking part in public affairs." It was used in this sense by Herodotus, Plato, Thucydides, and others. Then, it was an easy transition to the secondary meaning, namely, "one who has no professional knowledge, whether of politics or any other subject," in which sense it was used by Thucydides and others. Though the term was variously applied, these were its leading senses in the Greek language. After making its appearance in the English language, in which it is still a Greek word, merely Anglicized, it had a similar history, and retained, for a time, the same meanings which it had in Greek usage. These meanings, though current in the English of three hundred years ago, are now obsolete. According to Webster, the word has had the following meanings: 1. "A man in private station, as distinguished from

37

one holding public office." It was thus used by Jeremy Taylor in the seventeenth century in the following sentence: "Humility is a duty in great ones, as well as in idiots;" and by the same author in the sentence: "St. Austin affirmed that the plain places of Scripture are sufficient to all laics, and all idiots or private persons." 2. In its second stage in English, Webster says it meant: "An unlearned, ignorant, or simple person, as distinguished from the educated." It was used in this sense by writers of English three hundred years ago. The following passage from Charles Blount, a deistical writer of the seventeenth century, is cited by Webster as an instance of this usage: "Christ was received of idiots, of the vulgar people, and of the simpler sort, while he was rejected, despised and persecuted even unto death by the high priests, lawyers, scribes, doctors, and rabbis."

Thus far the English usage of this Anglicized Greek word, the reader can see, is parallel with its Greek usage; but at this point, it took on another meaning in English usage, which is: "A human being destitute of the ordinary intellectual powers, whether congenital, developmental, or accidental; commonly, a person without understanding from birth." It was, of course, an easy step to this last meaning, since the word had long been used to denote either a private person, hence one more obscure than those in public life, or an unlearned or simple person. The word has now entirely lost these latter meanings, and it is used almost universally to denote "a person without understanding from birth." The only exceptions are when it is sometimes used as a term of reproach. It is still in process of change, and this latter may in time become its established meaning.

9. The word *silly*. In this term, we find illustrated the fact that, under the influence of those principles which in the course of time bring about changes in a language, words sometimes completely reverse their meaning. This very familiar word "silly" is nothing more nor less than a corruption of the Anglo-Saxon or Old English *sælig,* which meant *happy* or *fortunate;* and this again is from *sæl,* which meant *good.* The term is said to be akin to the Latin *sollus,* meaning "whole," and the Greek ὅλος (*holos*), having the same meaning. Hence, "silly" in English originally meant "happy, fortunate, blessed," and was so used in the fifteenth century. From this it came to mean "harmless, innocent;" then, "weak, helpless, frail;" and at the time of Shakespeare and Milton it meant "rustic, plain, simple." From this, there was an easy transition to the present meaning of the word which, according to Webster, is: "Weak in intellect; destitute of ordinary strength of mind; foolish; simple;" or, "proceeding from want of understanding or common judgment; characterized by weakness or folly; unwise; absurd; stupid; as, silly conduct; a silly question." Hence, to speak of a man in the fifteenth century as "silly" was to say

that he was *happy;* but to use the term now, as my readers well know, is to convey a vastly different meaning.

10. The word *alderman.* This word, composed of the terms "elder" and "man," has retained almost entirely its Anglo-Saxon form. It not only meant originally "a senior or superior; a person of rank or dignity;" but it implied one of "superior wisdom or authority," such as princes, dukes, earls, and archbishops, and meant in England one who was second only to the king. Through the evolution of centuries, the term has lost much in prestige and dignity until an "alderman," in present-day English, is no more than "one of a board or body of municipal officers next in order to the mayor and having a legislative function."

Now, that the Greek Language was influenced, in a marked degree, by this evolutionary principle is so well attested by all classes of scholars, without exception, who have spoken on the subject, that a few representative quotations will be all that is necessary on this point. Furthermore, as the present treatise is vitally concerned with the Greek of the New Testament period, and particularly with the fact that the language had undergone many changes at that time as compared with its status in the classic period, we shall quote from those who have made the Greek of the New Testament, and other Greek of that period, a specialty.

1. Dr. George Benedict Winer, in his renowned Grammar of the Greek Testament, says:

In the age of Alexander the Great and his successors the Greek language underwent an internal change of a double nature. On the one hand, a literary prose language was formed, which was founded on the Attic dialect, yet differed from it by adopting a common Greek element, and even admitting numerous provincialisms (ἡ κοινὴ or ἑλληνικὴ διάλεκτος). On the other hand, a popular spoken language arose, in which the previously distinct dialects spoken by the various Greek tribes were blended, with a predominance of the Macedonic variety. This latter compound, varying in some respects in the various provinces of Asia and Africa subjected to the Macedonian rule, constitutes the special foundation of the diction of the New Testament, as it does also of the Septuagint and Apocrypha.—*New Testament Grammar,* p. 20.

2. Alexander Buttman, in his Grammar of the New Testament Greek, speaking in general terms of the changes that were constantly going on in the Greek language throughout its history, says:

Frequently it has been desirable to bring into prominence the agreement between the New Testament language and ordinary Greek usage, particularly in those cases where such agreement appears rather as exceptional, and a departure from the usage of the New Testament elsewhere. Moreover, the usage of the classic authors themselves varies so much, according to time, place, subject, etc., that it could not fail often to seem appropriate to indicate the New Testament usage and this or that department of classic Greek.—*Grammar of the New Testament Greek*, p. 76.

3. JAMES HOPE MOULTON, in the brilliant *Prolegomena* of his Grammar of New Testament Greek, makes the following interesting statement:

We are now ready to inquire how this Common Greek of the New Testament rose out of the classical language. Some features of its development are undoubted, and may be noted first. The impulse which produced it lay, beyond question, in the work of Alexander the Great. The unification of Hellas was a necessary first step in the accomplishment of his dream of Hellenizing the world which he had marked out for conquest. To achieve unity of speech throughout the little country which his father's diplomatic and military triumphs had virtually conquered for him, was a task too serious for Alexander himself to face. But unconsciously he effected this, as a by-product of his colossal achievement; and the next generation found that not only had a common language emerged from the chaos of Hellenic dialects, but a new and nearly homogeneous world-speech had been created, in which Persian and Egyptian might do business together, and Roman proconsuls issue their commands to the subjects of a mightier empire than Alexander's own. His army was in itself a powerful agent in the leveling process which ultimately destroyed nearly all the Greek dialects. The Anabasis of the Ten Thousand Greeks, seventy years before, had doubtless produced results of the same kind on a small scale.—*Prolegomena*, pp. 30. 31.

The same author, in another work entitled, "An Introduction to the Study of New Testament Greek," says:

It need hardly be added that gradual changes in the vocabulary were going on steadily through the whole period which leads up to our era. That force of spoken language which is always weakening old words and bringing in new expressions to be toned down in their turn, was acting as powerfully in Greek as it does now in English; and in the course of centuries the undignified or exaggerated character of a word or phrase would be entirely forgotten.—*Introduction*, p. 9.

4. Dr. Adolph Deissman, the brilliant Professor of New Testament Exegesis in the University of Heidelberg, in his recent work, "New Light on the New Testament," says:

The historical investigation of the language of the New Testament is still in its infancy, but we are already in a position to say that it has shown the New Testament to be, speaking generally, a specimen of the colloquial form of late Greek, and of the popular colloquial language in particular.—*New Light on the New Testament*, p. 34.

5. Charles Louis Loos, Professor (*Emeritus*) of the Greek Language and Literature in Transylvania University, who has been a successful student and teacher of both New Testament and classic Greek for more than half a century, in an able article on New

Testament Greek in the Christian Quarterly Review, says:

But by far the most important changes and which interest us most, are those which refer to new or modified meanings given to already existing and current Greek words, whether in the old classic or in the new postclassic Greek. It is these changes which especially concern us in the study of the New Testament.—*Quarterly* for 1884, p. 21.

Now in the light of the well-established principles of philology which have been disclosed in this chapter, my readers must be prepared to see not only the reasonableness of our contention that *psallo* (ψάλλω) has had widely different meanings in the different periods of its history, but also how and why it is that the lexicons tell us, as we have seen, that it means to pluck the hair, to twang the bowstring, to twitch a carpenter's line, to touch the chords of a musical instrument or to make instrumental music, and to touch the chords of the human heart or to sing. They can also see that just as the English words "resent," "candidate," "animosity," "prevent," "lewd," "silly," "idiot," and many others, once had meanings that are now entirely obsolete and not even known to the average speaker or writer of English to-day, so the Greek word *psallo* (ψάλλω) once meant to pluck the hair, twang the bowstring, twitch a carpenter's line, and to touch the chords of a musical instrument, but had entirely lost all of these meanings before the beginning of the New Testament period, and that, therefore, the word is never used in the New Testament nor in cotemporaneous literature in any of these senses. At this time, it not only meant to sing, but that is the only sense in which it was used, all the other meanings having entirely disappeared.

CHAPTER V.

Psallo as Affected by the Law of Evolution with More from the Lexicons.

We have seen that the philological principles presented in preceding chapters are characteristic alike of all living languages, and hence that the Greek language is no exception to the rule. In further confirmation of this fact, we now propose to show, from the highest lexical authority, that these principles are particularly exemplified in the word *psallo* (ψάλλω).

In the Preface to their renowned lexicon, referring to the different periods covered by the authors they cite, Liddell and Scott, to quote in part their language again, say: "The date of each author's 'floruit' is added in the margin; and by comparing this with the short summary of the chief Epochs of Greek Literature prefixed to the Catalogue, it will be easy to determine the time of a word's first usage, and of its subsequent changes of signification;" and, with still greater significance, they declare that "the Language changed differently in different places at the same time," in proof of which they found themselves compelled, as we have already observed in another chapter, to place Demosthenes and Aristotle in different Epochs.

Hence, from all the facts now before us, even granting that the word *psallo* (ψάλλω) was used in a given sense at one time, it would not follow that the same idea was perpetuated in the word without change. Whether it was or was not so perpetuated, is a question for decision upon its own merits. What, now, are the facts relating to this point? Is there any evidence that *psallo* (ψάλλω) was, in any way, affected by these evolutionary principles? We shall allow the Lexicons themselves to answer:

1. The Greek lexicon of Sophocles, himself a native Greek and for thirty-eight years Professor of the Greek Language in Harvard University, covers all of the Roman period and the Byzantine period down to the end of the eleventh century, in all more than twelve hundred years' history of the language from B.C. 146 to A.D. 1100. As the basis of his monumental work, this profound and tireless scholar examined, as we have found by actual count, 146 secular and 77 ecclesiastical authors of the Roman period, and 109 secular and 262 ecclesiastical, modern Greek, and scholastic authors of the Byzantine period, a grand total of 594 authors and covering a period of more than twelve hundred years, and he declares that there is not a single example of *psallo* (ψάλλω) throughout this long period involving or implying the use of an instrument, but says that it meant always and everywhere "*to chant, sing* religious hymns."

2. The Greek lexicon of Thayer which, by the

47

unanimous testimony of modern scholarship, now occupies the very highest place in the field of New Testament lexicography, although specially devoted to New Testament Greek, often gives the classical meaning of words. Accordingly, in harmony with the classical lexicons, as we have already seen, he says the word meant to pluck or pull, as the hair; to twang the bowstring; to touch the chords of a musical instrument, and hence to play instrumental music; but, in citing authorities in confirmation of these meanings, it is a significant fact that he is compelled, with the other lexicographers, to go back to the same periods of the language prior to New Testament times to which they appealed for the same purpose, and he cites some of the same authorities cited by Liddell and Scott; *but when this prince of New Testament lexicographers comes to the New Testament period, he omits all of these meanings, and limits it to touching the chords of the human heart,* saying that it means "IN THE NEW TESTAMENT TO SING A HYMN, CELEBRATE THE PRAISES OF GOD IN SONG." Then, as if to put an end to the controversy, the great lexicon of Sophocles, devoted exclusively to the Roman and Byzantine periods, and thus covering the entire period of New Testament and patristic literature, says he found not a single example of the word having any other meaning.

We may now regard it as an established fact, vouched for by the very highest lexical authority, that in the course of centuries the term *psallo* (ψάλλω underwent several complete changes in meaning, although, as we have already seen, its one radical idea, *"to touch,"* runs through all its varied uses and applications; and that at the opening of the New Testament period, its ancient meanings, to pluck or pull the hair, to twang the bowstring, and to touch the chords of a musical instrument, were as completely gone from the word as *"to be happy"* is now gone from the word "silly," or *"private citizen"* from the word "idiot."

We here introduce some illustrative examples of the use of *psallo* outside of the New Testament and after it had acquired the meaning simply *to sing,* and we select them from the Christian Fathers. Chrysostom and Theodoret lived, respectively, during the latter half of the fourth century and the first half of the fifth century, A.D., the former having been born in Antioch, Syria, in the year 347, and the latter having been born in the same city about the year 387, or near the close of the fourth century. Commenting on Ephesians 5: 19, Chrysostom says:

Dost thou wish, he says, to be cheerful? Dost thou wish to employ the day? I give the spiritual drink; for drunkenness even cuts off the articulate sound of our tongue; it makes us lisp and stammer, and distorts the eyes, and the whole frame together. Learn to sing psalms (μάθε ψάλλειν), and thou shalt see the delightfulness of the employment. For they who sing psalms (οἱ ψάλλοντες) are filled with the Holy Spirit, as they who sing (οἱ ᾄδοντες) Satanic songs are filled with an unclean spirit. What is meant by,

49

with your hearts to the Lord? It means, with close attention and understanding. For they who do not attend closely merely sing (ἁπλῶς ψάλλουσι), uttering the words, whilst their heart is roaming elsewhere.— *The Nicene and Post-Nicene Fathers,* Vol. XIII., Homily XIX., p. 138.*

We accept the foregoing translation with the observation that, to be uniform, *psallo,* in all of its occurrences in the passage, should be rendered the same way. In the first and second, it is rendered "sing psalms;" and in the third, "sing." However, the fact of simply *singing* is preserved in each instance, and this is the vital point.

Now, here is an instance of the use of *psallo* in which the context clearly shows that it can have no other meaning but to sing. After saying, "They who do not attend closely, *merely 'psallo'* " (ἁπλῶς ψάλλουσι), he adds the explanatory clause, "uttering the words" (τὰ ῥήματα φθεγγόμενοι), showing, beyond all just ground for doubt, that, with Chrysostom, "*to psallo*" was *to use the organs of speech,* which, of

---

* For the benefit of any reader who may desire it, we here transcribe the Greek of the passage from Chrysostom:—" Βούλει, φησὶν, εὐφαίνεσθαι; βούλει τὴν ἡμέραν ἀλισκειν; Ἐγώ σοι δίδωμι πότον πνευμάτικον. Ἡ γὰρ μέθη καὶ τὴν εὔσημον ἐκκόπτει φωνὴν τῆς γλώσσης τῆς ἡμετέρας ψελλίζειν παρασκευάζουσα, καὶ ὀφθαλμοὺς καὶ πάντα ἁπλῶς διαστρέφουσα. Μάθε ψάλλειν, καὶ ὄψει τοῦ πράγματος τὴν ἡδονήν. Οἱ ψάλλοντες γὰρ πνεύματος πληροῦνται ἁγίου, ὥσπερ οἱ ᾁδοντες τὰς σατανικὰς ᾠδὰς, πνεύματος ἀκαθάρτου. Τί ἐστιν, ' ἐν ταῖς καρδίαις ὑμῶν τῷ κυρίῳ; Τουτέστι, μετὰ συνέσεως προσέχοντες· οἱ γὰρ οὐ προσέχοντες, ἁπλῶς ψάλλουσι, τὰ ῥήματα φθεγγομενοι, τῆς καρδίας ῥεμβομένης ἑτέρωθι.''—*Chrysostom's Homilies on Ephesians, 5: 19, London Edition, 1852.*

course, might be going on while the "heart is roaming elsewhere;" but that, to be acceptable, it must be such an "uttering of words" as *touches the chords of the heart,* or comes from the heart.

We have a similar example from Theodoret. This eminent ecclesiastic of the fifth century, commenting on Eph. 5: 19, says:

For not only does he make melody (ψάλλει) in his heart who moves his tongue, but he who excites his mind to the understanding of the things said.—*Commentary on Ephesians, London Edition, 1870.**

Thus, according to Theodoret, *"to psallo"* is to "move the tongue"—that is, to utter words in song, and so to utter them as to excite the mind "to the understanding of the things said." This is in perfect accord with Paul's use of the word in New Testament times when he says: "I will sing (ψαλῶ) with the understanding (τῷ νοί) also."†

Here we have clear and conclusive proof that in the New Testament period and at the time of Theodoret, nearly five hundred years later, the word meant simply to sing. This is the reason why the lexicon of Sophocles covering these periods, but not the classic period, gives no other definition of the word.

Hence, the conclusion is inevitable that one would be just as consistent to take the position that "silly"

---

*The following is the original of the passage: " Τῇ καρδίᾳ γὰρ ψάλλει ὁ μὴ μόνον τὴν γλῶτταν κινῶν, ἀλλὰ καὶ τὸν νοῦν εἰς τὴν τῶν λεγομένων κατανόησιν διεγείρων."—*London Edition, 1870.*

†ψαλῶ τῷ πνεύματι, ψαλῶ δὲ καὶ τῷ νοί.—1 Cor. 14: 15.

now means *"to be happy,"* and that *"*idiot*"* means a *"private citizen,"* and then, in proof of it, to appeal to these definitions as given in the English dictionaries, as one is to take the position that *psallo* (ψάλλω) in the New Testament means to play instrumental music, and then, in proof of it, to appeal to this definition as given in the Greek dictionaries. If not, why not? The cases are precisely parallel. We are simply confronted with the fact that the greatest New Testament Greek Lexicon in existence gives *"to play on a stringed instrument"* as a meaning of *psallo* (ψάλλω) precisely as the greatest English dictionary in existence gives *"happy"* and *"fortunate"* as meanings of *"silly,"* and *"private citizen"* as a meaning of *"idiot."*

It goes without saying, therefore, that those who quote Greek lexicons on *psallo* (ψάλλω), or any other word with a similar history, without carefully observing this distinction are both confusing and misleading in their use of such authorities; and yet this is precisely what is sometimes done in the case of this particular word. We have ready at hand a remarkable and significant instance in illustration. Professor Clinton Lockhart, who at the time referred to was a Professor in Drake University, but is now President of Christian University; J. B. Briney, at the time Editor of the Christian Companion; and W. K. Homan, at the time Editor of the Christian Courier, furnish a remarkable coincidence in their manner of quoting from Thayer's Greek Lexicon on this

52

word. We first give Thayer's definition of *psallo* (ψάλλω) in full, which is as follows:

Ψάλλω (from ψάω, to rub, wipe; to handle, touch); a. *to pluck off, pull out:* ἔθειραν, the hair. b. *to cause to vibrate by touching, to twang;* specifically χόρδην, *to touch* or *strike the chord, to twang the strings* of a musical instrument so that they gently vibrate; and absolutely *to play on a stringed instrument, to play the harp,* etc.; Septuagint for *niggēn* and much oftener for *zimmēr to sing to the music of the harp;* in the New Testament *to sing a hymn, to celebrate the praises of God in song.*

That is his definition *verbatim* and in full, without giving his list of references to either the classic authors or the New Testament.

Now, for the coincidence before mentioned. Professor Lockhart quoted Thayer's definition as follows:

Thayer's Greek-English Lexicon of the New Testament (the latest and largest New Testament lexicon in the English language): "*Psallo*—from *psao,* to rub, wipe; to handle, touch; to pluck off, pull out the hair; to cause to vibrate by touching; to twang; especially to touch or strike the chord; to twang the strings of a musical instrument; to play the harp, etc. Septuagint, for *niggēn,* piel form of *nagan,* and much oftener for *zimmēr,* piel form of *zamar*—to sing to the music of the harp."—*Stark-Warlick Debate,* p. 99.

He omitted the phrase, "IN THE NEW TESTAMENT."

Editor Briney quoted it as follows:

Psallo as Affected by the Law of Evolution.

What is the meaning of the term psallo? As applied to music, Thayer's Greek-English Lexicon of the New Testament, gives the following answer: "To play a stringed instrument, to play the harp; to sing to the music of the harp; to sing a hymn, to celebrate the praise of God in song."—*Christian Companion*, February 15, 1905, p. 4.

He omitted the phrase, "IN THE NEW TESTAMENT."

Editor Homan quoted it as follows:

Professor Carr denies that psallo of itself carries the idea of an instrumental accompaniment to the singing. Well, the determination of this point is not essential to the settlement of the right to use the instrument, but it so happens that Professor Carr is at variance with the leading commentators and Greek lexicons. . . . Thayer's New Testament Lexicon: "Psallo: to rub, to wipe; to handle, to touch; to pluck off, pull out; to cause to vibrate by touching; to twang, to touch or strike the chord, to twang the strings of a musical instrument so that it shall gently vibrate, and in an absolute sense to play on a stringed instrument, to play the harp, etc. To sing to the music of the harp, to sing a hymn, to celebrate the praises of God in song."—*The Christian Courier*, February 14, 1907, p. 6.

He omitted the phrase, "IN THE NEW TESTAMENT."

Now, this omitted phrase, when left where Thayer placed it, marks the boundary line between what he gives as the classical meanings of *psallo*, on the one hand, and its New Testament meaning, on the other:

54

in the former he includes pulling out the hair and instrumental music as once signified by the word; in the latter he leaves out these meanings entirely. It is therefore unfortunate to omit the phrase when attempting to give Thayer's definition of *psallo* since this very material and significant distinction made by the author cannot otherwise be seen.

Leonard F. Bittle, for a number of years Editor of the Octographic Review, was a fine Greek scholar and gave much attention to this particular word. After extended research in the literature of the subject, he wrote the following as his deliberate conviction and conclusion:

Psallo, according to the best authorities, is derived from *psao,* and is in fact merely a strengthened form of this root word. Robinson in his Greek and English Lexicon of the New Testament gives this account of it: "Psallo, future psalo (psao) to touch, to twitch, to pluck, e. g. the hair or beard, psall' etheiran (pluck up the beard) Æschyl. Pers. 1062; also a string, to twang, e. g. the string of a bow, *toxon neuran psallein* [to draw the bowstring.] Eurip. Bacch. 784."

This definition, in which the older and the later lexicographers agree with Robinson, shows that in its radical or primary sense the word psallo has no reference to music. But from drawing the chord of a bow to striking the strings of a harp was an easy transition, so *psallo* came at length to denote the latter act especially.

But as singing usually accompanied the playing of the harp the word *psallo* was made to include the vocal music also. And the transition did not stop here. The word *psallo* began to be used without reference to the instrument, and became a synonym of *ado,* I sing.

So Thomas Sheldon Green, in his New Testament Lexicon, after noticing the primary and secondary meanings of *psallo,* adds this definition: "In the New Testament* to sing praises, Rom. 15: 9; 1 Cor. 14: 15; Eph. 5: 19; Jas. 5: 13."

That this view of the matter is correct needs not many words to prove. Still for the sake of the doubting reader, we shall offer sundry reasons showing that the apostles, and other early Christians used *psallo* in the limited sense of singing or making vocal melody.

1. In the two parallel passages in which Paul exhorts his brethren to use psalms and hymns and spiritual songs instead of bacchanalian odes common among the heathen he expresses himself thus: "Be not drunk with wine wherein is excess, but be filled with the Spirit: speaking (*lalountes*) to yourselves in psalms and hymns, and spiritual songs, singing (*adontes*) and making melody (*psallontes*) in your heart to the Lord," Eph. 5: 19. "Let the word of Christ dwell in you richly in all wisdom; teaching and admonishing one another in psalms, and hymns and spiritual songs, singing (*adontes*) with grace in your hearts to the Lord." Col. 3: 16.

The Revised Version has "singing and making melody with your heart to the Lord." This is a better rendering, and excludes the idea of instrumental music entirely. Indeed the Common Version also excludes it. In writing to the Colossians Paul omits "making melody" (*psallontes*) and uses singing (*adontes*) only. The latter word includes the former, for singing is speaking words in a musical tone. * * *

3. They who say that *psallo* in the apostolic epis-

---

*The same phrase used by Thayer, and for the same purpose.

tles means singing with the harp, and thus sanctions the use of other instruments in worship take upon themselves the burden of proving that the primitive disciples universally, deliberately, and persistently disobeyed a plain commandment of the Lord,—that Paul told these disciples to play on the *harp* and they never did so in their assemblies.

4. The assumption that *psallo* means to play on the harp does not sanction the use of an entirely different instrument like an organ or French horn any more than the fact that Christ broke bread at the Passover sanctions the use of beef or pork in the Lord's Supper. When the Savior says, Remember me in the breaking of bread they disobey Him who try to remember Him sacramentally in the eating of meat. So if Paul says, Play on the harp, they set at naught his counsel who play on something else. To sum up—In its primary sense *psallo* had no reference to music at all, but meant merely to touch or twitch or pull; then it was used to denote the drawing of the bowstring in shooting arrows; afterwards it was restricted to making music on a harp by touching its strings; then it was applied to singing with the accompaniment of harp-music; finally it was used to denote singing psalms without any instrument save the organs of speech. In this last and latest sense it is used exclusively in the New Testament, and occurs only five times—Rom. 15: 9; 1 Cor. 14: 15 (twice); Eph. 5: 19; and Jas. 5: 13.

From the verb *psallo,* I sing, comes the noun *psalmos,* a psalm. This name was at first given to any poem sung to the notes of the harp. It was afterwards applied to the poem itself without reference to the instrument.

In the New Testament it is used *five* times in the

singular number—Luke 24: 44; Acts 13: 33; 1 Cor. 14: 26; Eph. 5: 19; and Col. 3: 16; and *two* times in the plural,—Luke 20: 42; and Acts 1: 20. Each time it denotes a sacred poem, but in what way this differed from a hymn or song is not clear.—*Octographic Review.*

Before leaving the lexicons, it is deemed proper to state, in this connection, that a number of unavailing attempts have been made, by overzealous advocates of instrumental music, to break the force of the great lexicons of Sophocles and Thayer on the meaning of *psallo.* George P. Slade, whose tract on the meaning of this Greek verb was published thirty years ago, soon after the appearance of Sophocles' great work, made an attempt to elicit from the learned author of the lexicon, who was then still living, something that would break or modify the force of what the lexicon says on this word; but the attempt met with a signal failure. For some reason, Brother Slade withheld from his tract his note of inquiry, and gave out only a part of the noted linguist's reply, which was as follows:

Cambridge, February 1, 1880.

Rev. G. P. Slade.

Dear Sir: My lexicon is intended for those who wish to read the authors of the *Roman and Byzantine* periods of the language. It presupposes a good knowledge of the preceding periods ('Alexandrian, Athenian, Ionic). . . . Yours truly,

E. A. SOPHOCLES.

—*Search for Truth Concerning Instrumental Music,* p. 21.

The dots at the close of the foregoing note indicate that something is omitted, but it may be safely assumed that Brother Slade omitted nothing that would favor the use of instrumental music in the worship. Hence, as the matter stands, the reply of the eminent Harvard Professor gave forth nothing in support of any other meaning of *psallo* than that given in his lexicon.

But Brother Slade makes this comment: "The Lexicons previously quoted embrace *all* periods of the *dead language;* Sophocles' Lexicon presupposes this knowledge, and no one would expect to find it in his Lexicon." But any one, who thinks properly, "would expect to find," in a lexicon made for a given period, *the full and complete meaning assigned to a word which it really had during that period.* It would be a poor lexicon that did not do this. The statement in Sophocles' note that his lexicon "presupposes a good knowledge of the preceding periods" merely means what it says, and it certainly does *not* say, and does not mean, that the definitions of words in his lexicon are not *correct and complete* FOR THE PERIODS WHICH IT COVERS. And here is a most significant fact. If Sophocles' lexicon were a general lexicon of the Greek Language, such as that of Liddell and Scott, and were not confined to certain periods of the language, we might expect to find, and doubtless would find in it, the same classical meanings of *psallo,* such as to "pull the hair," "to twang the bowstring," "to twitch a carpenter's line," and "to make instrumental music," as are found in Liddell and Scott and other lexicons of similar scope. But the lexicon of Sophocles is limited to the *Roman and Byzantine* periods, including, in fact, only so much of the latter as to the end of the eleventh century, A.D. In other words, it covers the period from B.C. 146 to A.D. 1100. But we have already seen that before the beginning of the Roman period, i. e. B.C. 146, the above-mentioned classical meanings were no longer current in the language, and of course a lexicon limited to a time when *psallo* had no such meanings could not correctly say that it had them at that time. For this reason, they do not appear in Sophocles' lexicon at all.

We close this line of evidence with the strong testimony of DR. JAMES BEGG who, in his work entitled, "The Use of Organs," says of the word *psallo:*

This attempt to fix the meaning of the word as implying playing instead of singing, as used by the New Testament writers, was thoroughly set aside by Dr. Porteous, by a variety of evidence, one part of which is thus concluded: "From these quotations from the Greek fathers, the three first of whom flourished in the fourth century—men of great erudition, well skilled in the phraseology and language of Scripture, perfectly masters of the Greek tongue, which was then written and spoken with purity in the countries where they resided; men, too, who for conscience' sake would not handle the word of God deceitfully, it is evident that the Greek word ψάλλω signified in their time singing with the voice alone.

PSALLO AS AFFECTED BY THE LAW OF EVOLUTION.

* * * In regard to the verb itself, besides the passage in James and in Eph. 5: 19, just referred to, ψάλλω only occurs *three* times in the New Testament; *twice* (1 Cor. 14: 15), where its use absolutely excludes instrumental music, and must imply singing inspired (?) songs or psalms—'I will sing with the spirit, and I will sing with the understanding also;' and *once* (Rom. 15: 9), 'As it is written, For this cause I will confess to thee among the Gentiles, and sing unto thy name.' It is interesting to notice that the latter passage is exactly copied from the Septuagint (Psa. 18: 49), and this affords striking proof of the correctness of the rendering for which we are now contending. As thus quoted by the apostle, we have an inspired rendering into the Greek verb ψάλλω of a Hebrew word which is usually translated 'sing praises' or 'sing psalms.' 'Singing psalms' was the only authorized vocal praise of the church of old. The question now, as every one knows, is not about the roots or the original meaning of words, but about the sense in which they were used by the inspired writers; ψάλλω never occurs in the New Testament, in its radical signification, to strike or play upon an instrument."—Cited by Girardeau, *"Music in the Church,"* pp. 116-118.

CHAPTER VI.

Psallo with a Significant Parallel.

In our familiar words "touch" and "strike" which, according to the testimony of all the lexicons, exactly express the radical and primary meaning of *psallo* (ψάλλω), there is an almost exact parallel in their usage in English Literature with the usage of *psallo* (ψάλλω) in Greek Literature. In Webster's twelfth and thirteenth definitions of "touch," he gives: "to play on; as, to touch an instrument of music; to perform, as a tune; to play." In justification of this, he gives us Milton's rhythmic line: "They *touched* their golden harps," and the graphic words of Sir Walter Scott: "A person in the royal retinue *touched* a light and lively air on the flageolet." Then, to the same point are the words of England's greatest bard: "Soft stillness and the night become the *touches* of sweet harmony," meaning, of course, the *musical notes* or *sounds* of sweet harmony. Under the word "strike," the phrase, "to strike up," is defined by the same world-renowned authority as meaning "to commence to play, as a musician; to begin to sound, as an instrument."

Now, out of the eighteen meanings of the word "touch," and the twenty-one of the word "strike,"

62

as given by this standard authority, how are we to
determine the meaning of these terms when we meet
them in literature? Shall we select one meaning
and force it upon the word whenever and wherever
we find an example of it to the exclusion of all the
other meanings? If not, why not? For instance,
because I find that the English word "touch," like
the Greek ψάλλω, means to play on an instrument of
music, shall I conclude that wherever I find an oc-
currence of the word, I have found instrumental music? If so, then when we read in the daily papers,
or in some book, that an orator delivered a *touching* discourse, the good ship Germania *touched* at
Queenstown, or of John Dryden's advice to an artist,
"Never give the least *touch* with your pencil till you
have well examined your design," we must understand, of course, that the orator made *instrumental
music* with his discourse, that the Germania made
instrumental music at Queenstown, and that the one-
time poet laureate of England advises the artist not
to make *instrumental music* with his pencil till he
has well examined his design! This is precisely the
course of reasoning pursued by those who falla-
ciously conclude that because they find the word
psallo (ψάλλω) in the New Testament, they have necessarily found instrumental music. Why not conclude, as intimated in a previous chapter, that they
have found "plucking the hair," "twanging the bowstring," or "twitching the carpenter's line?" The
word has had all these meanings, and the standard

lexicons so declare. Such reasoning violates one of the fundamental principles of all interpretation in at least two particulars: 1. It ignores the fact that words not only often completely change their meaning in the course of time, but often have a variety of applied meanings at the same time. 2. It is in total disregard of the context, a principle, the importance of which is recognized by all reliable authorities in exegesis. Governed by these sound principles of interpretation, no one ever has any difficulty in understanding the words "touch" and "strike" in English literature, nor the word *psallo* (ψάλλω) in Greek literature.

From the premises thus far submitted, even if it were a fact that the word under review had not undergone any change of meaning at the opening of the New Testament period, still those who claim that a given passage authorizes instrumental music because it contains the word *psallo* (ψάλλω), are guilty of the *petitio principii,* or the fallacy of *begging the question.* They assume the very point in dispute by assuming that the use of a musical instrument *inheres* in the word. *No lexicographer known to the author has ever so claimed.* The fallacy which lurks here has done much mischief, and the author respectfully engages here and now to expose it with a simple statement of incontestable facts.

We here introduce another interesting parallel. In the light of usage as reflected in the lexicons, the instrument no more inheres in *psallo* (ψάλλω) than

64

water does in *baptizo* (βαπτίζω). In fact, at this point there is an interesting analogy between the two words. You can *baptize* without water, and you can *psallo* without an instrument of music. Βαπτίζω means to dip or immerse, regardless of the particular element in which the action takes place, and the word ψάλλω means to touch or strike, regardless of the particular object touched or struck. These are the inherent ideas in these words running through all their varied uses, and they are the key to the meaning in every instance whether the word be used literally or metaphorically. Water does not inhere in βαπτίζω, nor does an instrument of music in ψάλλω. When we meet with the word βαπτίζω in Greek literature we have to learn from the context, or from some other source than the word itself, what the element is in which the action takes place. It may be water, it may be fire, it may be the Holy Spirit, it may be suffering, or it may be some other element, the element itself never inhering in the word. So precisely when we meet with the word ψάλλω, the word itself does not indicate the object touched, or the instrument used. It may be the hair or beard, it may be a carpenter's line, it may be a bowstring, it may be a harp or other instrument of music, or, metaphorically, it may be the human heart. If we *psallo* with a bowstring, that is the instrument; if with a carpenter's line, that is the instrument; if with a harp, guitar, or organ, that is the instrument; and if with the human heart, that is the instrument.

Thus, the context of a word, or the time when, and sometimes the place where, it was used, is often the only means of determining its import; and, touching the New Testament usage and meaning of *psallo* in particular, it specifically says that Christians are to *"psallo with the heart"* (ψάλλοντες τῇ καρδίᾳ ὑμῶν, *making melody with your heart,* Eph. 5: 19). This is the only *"psalloing"* mentioned in its inspired pages, and therein incorporated as a part of Christian worship.

CHAPTER VII.

Facts Accounting for Differences Among the Lexicographers.

In the light of such an array of facts as we now have before us, the very pertinent question arises, Why are there any differences at all among the lexicographers? We reply, for the same reason, and in precisely the same way, that we find differences among them on βαπτίζω. In fact, this word and the word ψάλλω, between which we have already seen an interesting analogy, present an equally interesting parallel in the treatment which they have received at the hands of the theological world. This may be seen from the following considerations:

1. There *are no differences* among lexicographers and theologians as to the classical meaning of either of these words. They all agree that βαπτίζω in classic Greek meant to dip or immerse, and that from the time of Aristophanes B.C. 450 to that of Dionysius, of Halicarnassus, a period of about four hundred years, the word ψάλλω meant to pluck, as the hair or beard, to twang the bowstring, to twitch a carpenter's line, and to touch the chords of a musical instrument.

2. In like manner, they all agree that, at the open-

ing of the New Testament period, ψάλλω had come to mean to sing, and that it is so used in the New Testament.

3. The one point of divergence is that *some* of them have ventured to say that the word, in the New Testament, involves the use of the instrument; yet the very highest authorities among them in New Testament Greek and all other Greek covering the New Testament period—authorities devoted exclusively to the Greek of that period, declare that, in the New Testament and in all patristic literature, it meant simply to sing.

Now, for a significant coincidence. It so happens that those lexicographers who have ventured to say that ψάλλω, in the New Testament, means to make instrumental music, are the very same lexicographers who have ventured to say that βαπτίζω means "to pour." The four illustrious names which appear on this roll are Henry George Liddell, Robert Scott, John Parkhurst, and Edward Robinson, the first three of whom were of the Church of England, and the last a Presbyterian. The religious bodies with which these scholars were affiliated were prominent in their advocacy of pouring and sprinkling for baptism, and equally so in their use of instrumental music in the worship. Liddell and Scott would doubtless never have thought of "pour" as a meaning of βαπτίζω had it not been for their position and practice in the theological world. In the first London and first American edition of their lexicon they gave *"to pour upon"* as a meaning of βαπτίζω, but in the very next edition they expunged this definition as inadmissible, and it has remained expunged from all subsequent editions even down to the Eighth, which is the last and greatest edition of their famous work. But if they could be influenced, on theological grounds, to introduce, as a meaning of βαπτίζω, that which was really *never its meaning in any age,* how much more would they be liable, on the same grounds, to introduce, as a meaning of ψάλλω, that which *was* at one time one of its meanings? So thoroughly was Mr. Robinson under this influence that, failing to find in the classics any support for his theological position on βαπτίζω, he sought to find it in New Testament examples of the word which he fancied were not suitable to the idea of immersion; but in this effort to save his theology, he had to sacrifice his logic, for even granting that some passage is not suitable to the idea of immersion, it would certainly not follow that it favored either pouring or sprinkling. All this only shows that great learning in the languages combined with vast research in Biblical literature does not always overcome theological bias. The latter has unfortunately played its part in translations of the Bible, in commentaries, in histories, and sometimes in lexicons.

Finally, if the word ψάλλω had been subjected to the same searching and widespread investigation to which the theological world has subjected βαπτίζω, I have not the remotest doubt that the classical lexicons, when they come to New Testament Greek and all other Greek of the same period and of all subsequent periods, would expunge the idea of a musical instrument from ψάλλω just as Liddell and Scott, as we have seen, were compelled to expunge "pour" as a meaning of βαπτίζω. This conclusion finds strong confirmation in the fact that Joseph Henry Thayer, the author of the New Testament lexicon which, by the unanimous decision of present-day scholarship, stands not only at the head, but far above all other authorities in the special field of New Testament lexicography, was a Congregationalist; but, nevertheless, refused, as some others failed to do, to be influenced by theological considerations, and so put down, in his now famous lexicon, a faithful record of the true meaning of both these words.

CHAPTER VIII.

Scope of the Divine Command Authorizing Music in the Worship of God.

There are two kinds or classes of commands in the Holy Scriptures which are equally obligatory upon the children of God. For all practical purposes, we may distinguish them as GENERIC and SPECIFIC. In the sense here intended, a *generic* command is a command authorizing the performance of some act without giving directions as to the manner or method of its performance, while a *specific* command carries with it the manner or method of its performance. We shall see, however, that generic commands may become specific, and specific commands may become generic, according as they may be viewed in one relation or another. To illustrate: "Go" is a generic command, but either "ride" or "walk" is specific, each of them indicating a particular way or method of going. Furthermore, while in its relation to "go," the term "ride" is specific, still it is generic when viewed in relation to the different ways of riding, such as on boat, in a railway car, in a buggy, on horseback, etc. Thus, riding is both a *genus* and a *species*—a species when viewed in relation to "going,'' but a genus when viewed in relation to the different coördinate ways of riding.

The same principle of division and classification may be exemplified and illustrated in the animal kingdom. The term quadruped, for example, denotes a species of animal, but it denotes a genus in relation to horse. As a genus, it embraces the horse, cow, sheep, deer, and all other four-footed animals, but the term horse is more specific and embraces only a certain kind of four-footed animal, while animal, as a genus, embraces man and all other living beings of every variety.

The following diagram will illustrate the principle here before us:

ANIMAL

QUADRUPED				BIPED	
Horse	Cow	Sheep	Dog, etc.	Man	Bird, etc.
Different varieties	Different varieties	Different varieties	Different varieties	Different races	Different varieties

Now, from what has been said, and in the light of the foregoing diagram, it can readily be seen that if God should command His children to offer an animal sacrifice without any further specification, the command could be obeyed to the very letter of the law by offering any one of many kinds of animals. But, if the command should be more specific by naming *quadruped* as the particular kind of animal to be offered, while this would exclude all animals without four feet, it could, nevertheless, be strictly obeyed by offering any one of many kinds of four-footed animals. And if the command should proceed further on the descending scale and specify cow or ox as the animal to be offered, the circle or limits within which the command could be obeyed would be still further narrowed, and would exclude, not only all animals in general without four feet, but even all that have four feet except the cow or ox which, in that case, would be the particular four-footed animal named. Finally, if the command should descend to a still lower species and name a lamb one year old, or a red heifer without spot, as the animal to be offered, as was the case in some of the Old Testament sacrifices, the command would exclude all animals of every kind such as the horse, reindeer, sheep, or cow except the red heifer without spot and the lamb a year old. Even a heifer and a lamb, in such a case, would not do unless of the color and age prescribed. Quadruped, as the name signifies, includes all animals with four feet whether it be the horse, cow, sheep, goat, dog, deer, bear, buffalo, elephant, camel, or what not; but horse only includes every variety or species of horse, and cow every variety or species of cow.

If the illustration of our principle were taken from the vegetable kingdom, it would exhibit the same facts and lead to the same conclusion. For example, tree, as a genus, includes all kinds of trees on the face of the whole earth, but oak is only a certain species of tree. When we view oak as a genus, it includes, not all kinds of trees, but all kinds of oak, such as Black oak, Bur oak, Chestnut oak, Line oak, Post oak, Red oak, Spanish oak, Water oak, White oak, Willow oak, etc. Under tree, as a genus, would range, as coördinate species, oak, maple, pine, cedar, ash, birch, hickory, poplar, olive, dogwood, elm, etc. Any one of these species viewed as a genus would include only its own particular kind, and would exclude everything belonging to any other one of the several coördinate species. For example, Maple would include Common Maple, Sugar Maple, Water Maple, and every other kind of Maple, but it would include nothing belonging to Oak, Pine, Ash, Birch, or any other coördinate species. The following diagram will illustrate the principle:

TREE			
Oak	Maple	Pine	Ash
White, black, red, live, post, etc.	Common, sugar, water, etc.	White, red, Georgia, yellow, etc.	Mountain, white, etc.

Now, in view of this principle of generalization and division, it must be evident to the reader that any generic command of God involving merely *tree* for any purpose, could be kept strictly to the letter of the requirement by using any one of the many kinds of trees; whereas, if He should specifically command the use of oak, while this command could be literally kept by the use of any one of the several species of oak as well as another, still it could not be kept by using maple, pine, ash, or any other co-

74

ordinate species, or species of any other order. If God should say "tree" without further specification, then any kind of tree would fill the requirement, but if He should say "oak," then any kind of tree would not fill the requirement. If He should say "pine," then not only would it follow that any kind of tree would not do, but oak with all of its varieties would not do; nothing short of that particular kind of tree called "pine" would meet the demands of such a case. When God commanded Noah to make the Ark of gopher wood, that command excluded all kinds of wood except gopher. Of course if there were different varieties of gopher, any one or all of them could be used without transcending the limits of the divine command. However valuable other kinds of wood might be in the construction of the Ark, not one of them could be lawfully used under the directions which the Lord gave Noah. Not a single board, plank, beam, post, bar, or any other kind of piece of any other kind of wood could be used in making the Ark, except gopher. God said: "Make thee an Ark of gopher wood" (Gen. 6: 14). That settled the question once and forever with a man of Noah's faith and loyalty; and hence, the directions having been strictly followed, the historian says of this pious patriarch: "Thus did Noah; according to all that God commanded him, so did he" (Gen. 6: 22).

But it is equally evident that, if God had simply commanded Noah to make an Ark without specifying the kind of timber to be used, he would have been at liberty to use any kind whatever of which an Ark could be made. But if he had said, "Make it of oak," this would have excluded every other species of tree, such as pine, cedar, maple, etc.; yet he would have been at liberty to use any of the several kinds of oak; but if He had said, "Make it of White oak," then not only no other kind of tree outside of the oak family could have been lawfully used, but not even any of the oak family except White oak—the kind specified. In brief, if we would obey God, we must do the thing which God says, and not something else. "Ye are my friends, if ye do the things which I command you," Jno. 15: 14.

Now, I have been at particular pains to present somewhat at length this matter of generalization and division because of the vital and far-reaching principle involved. The sacredness and importance of this principle have been confirmed in every age of God's dealings with man from the day when Adam was placed in Eden to the close of John's vision on Patmos; and all that has been said in this chapter, in illustration of it, is to pave the way for the effort, now to be made, to ascertain the scope and meaning of the divine command which authorizes us to use music in the worship of God. That we may appreciate the principle in its application to this particular subject, let us suppose that God had merely commanded His people, in general terms, to make music in His praise. Now, keeping in view the principle of division and classification already before us, "music" is a generic term, and includes, not only all vocal and all instrumental music, but all the parts of both kinds, and all of the many kinds of instrumental music. Again, we may illustrate this important principle in a diagram, such as the following:

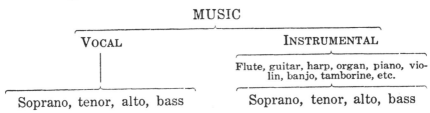

MUSIC

VOCAL   INSTRUMENTAL

                                         Flute, guitar, harp, organ, piano, violin, banjo, tamborine, etc.

Soprano, tenor, alto, bass   Soprano, tenor, alto, bass

Accordingly, if the command authorizing music in the worship of God had been given in the general terms just supposed, the conclusion would be inevitable that whether the music were vocal or instrumental, or whether it were on one kind of instrument or another, would be wholly immaterial, since each and all alike are embraced in the generic term "music;" and if we were making either vocal or instrumental music, or making the latter on any one or more of the numerous kinds of instruments, we would, in each and every case, be obeying the divine command. Reverting, for the moment, to our principle as formerly illustrated, we are commanded to "go" to men with the gospel; and whether we walk or ride, or whether we ride in one or another of the numerous ways of riding, we are, in each and every case, obeying the divine command to "go." But if we were commanded to "walk" to men with the gospel, all methods of going otherwise would be excluded, and we would be compelled to walk if we obeyed the command.

The same principle applies in precisely the same way to the religious organization under which, and through which, God's children are to work. If He had merely commanded them to work without giving them an organization through which, and under which, to work, with its divinely appointed board of supervisors and managers to look after the work, then they could obey the command by forming for themselves an organization for that purpose and appointing a board of supervisors to look after the work. But the Lord has given them an organization, and has specifically named its board of overseers and managers.

Now, turning to the word of God with renewed attention to our main theme, we find that Christians are nowhere commanded merely to *make music* in the praise of the Lord. This shows that it is not merely *music* that God wants in the worship, and that, if He wants music at all, it must be music of a special kind. Having seen that no generic term authorizing both vocal and instrumental music is used in the New Testament, we proceed now to the first division on the descending scale of classification and inquire, is there any term used which is more specific and which limits the music to one of these kinds, and if so, to which kind? It must be evident to ev-

78

ery thoughtful person that, in a case of two or more coördinate species, if God limits His command to one of the species, we do not obey that command when we use another; and if God has limited His directions for music in the worship to one of different coördinate kinds, we cannot be loyal to His directions without we limit our practice in the same way. If, for example, He has used a term or terms which mean instrumental music, then we are not following His directions when we sing or make vocal music; and, in like manner, if He has used a term or terms which mean vocal music, we are not following His directions when we make music of another kind. We inquire, then, what are the terms used? One fact is already settled, which the reader will please bear in mind, viz., both kinds are not commanded, for no generic term embracing both is used.

We now appeal, in the language of the ancient prophet, "to the law and to the testimony" (Isa. 8: 20), and the answer given by inspired men comes with no uncertain sound. The reader will please carefully note the terms used which indicate music. "And when they had sung a hymn, they went out unto the mount of Olives," Matt. 26: 30. "About midnight Paul and Silas were praying and singing hymns unto God, and the prisoners were listening to them," Acts 16: 25. "As it is written, Therefore will I give praise unto thee among the Gentiles, and sing unto thy name," Rom. 15: 9. "I will pray with the spirit, and I will pray with the understanding also; I will sing with the spirit, and I will sing with the understanding also,'' 1 Cor. 14: 15. ''Speaking one to another in psalms and hymns and spiritual songs, singing and making melody with your heart to the Lord,'' Eph. 5:19. ''Let the word of Christ dwell in you richly; in all wisdom teaching and admonishing one another with psalms and hymns and spiritual songs, singing with grace in your hearts unto God,'' Col. 3: 16. ''Is any among you suffering? let him pray. Is any cheerful? let him sing praise,'' Jas. 5: 13.

Thus, as expressed in the English language, the term ''sing'' is the term which is used by the Holy Spirit in giving directions as to the kind of music to be made in the praise of God. So certainly, therefore, as the term ''sing'' means to make vocal music, so certainly is vocal music the music which is divinely authorized for use in Christian worship. Of course in order to be logical at this point, as the author is well aware, it must be assumed that ''sing'' is a correct rendering of the original word or words used by the Holy Spirit, but he does not pause to discuss this question here since it is abundantly treated in other parts of this work. On the hypothesis, therefore, that ''sing'' is a correct rendering of the original, which is supported by the King James translators of 1611, the Revisers of 1881, and the very highest present-day authority, we are now prepared to appreciate the argument based upon this word.

We may observe, first of all, that whatever is necessarily involved in the command to sing is divinely authorized. For example, pitching the voice is necessarily involved in this command, and hence pitching the voice is divinely authorized. The reader will please note the fact that pitching the voice, in this case, is not a matter of indifference which may be had or omitted as one may like in obeying the command to sing, but it is an indispensable thing in singing—a thing without which singing cannot be had, without which the divine command cannot be obeyed. Pitching the voice is, therefore, divinely authorized in the divine command to sing.

Now, from these premises, it necessarily follows that, if there are different ways of pitching the tune, any one or all of them are divinely authorized, unless it be true that God has named some special way for it to be done. If He has, then we must do it that way if we would obey God. But we find no such special way of pitching the tune divinely ordained; and hence, being divinely commanded to sing, which necessarily involves pitching the tune, we are, therefore, by this very term, divinely authorized to pitch the tune, and to pitch it in any way by which it can be done, provided the particular way selected does not contravene God's law at some other point.

In Matt. 26: 30, as we have seen, we are informed that the Master and His disciples "sung a hymn;" in Acts 16: 25 that "Paul and Silas were praying and singing hymns unto God;" and in Eph. 5: 19

and Col. 3: 16, that "psalms, hymns, and spiritual songs" are the compositions to be used in "singing with grace in the heart unto God." Now, we not only learn here the character of compositions in general which Christians are to use in their worship, but we are told in particular that such compositions must be "spiritual." Here, now, is a new element, a new restriction or limitation introduced which must be observed in obeying the admonition to sing unto God. We are not merely commanded to "sing songs," but they must be "spiritual songs." Hence, although Christians, as we have seen, are admonished to sing, yet they may *sing* and not only *not* be obeying the divine admonition, but may be in actual *disobedience to God*. They cannot observe the divine admonition without singing songs, but they may sing songs without observing the divine admonition. The latter not only requires that they sing songs, but that they sing "spiritual songs."

Again, from the passages under review, we discover still another restriction or limitation. In their "singing unto God," Christians are to "speak one to another," and to "teach and admonish one another." From this it follows that the singing must be so conducted that those engaged in it not only "speak one to another," but so speak as to "teach and admonish one another." This clearly and definitely presents one of the divine purposes of the music appointed for Christian worship. It is to be music that instructs, music which communicates ideas from one to another, and which admonishes those engaged in it to right living. Nothing must interfere with this divine purpose. Any music which fails at this point, and to whatever extent it thus fails, is not pleasing to God, not being embraced within, but plainly excluded from, the scope of the divine command. Sometimes even vocal music, when those making it attempt to be artistic and entertaining rather than instructive and edifying, is such a failure.

Finally, the fact must never be overlooked that mere music, however artistic, bewitching, and enchanting, is not what the Lord ordained for His sublimely simple and holy worship. From all the testimony now before us, it clearly follows that music is not wanted by the Lord at all, except to assist in conveying and impressing thought, and music in Christian worship must be of this kind if those engaging in it would please Him. The spiritual compositions which we have seen Christians may sing in the worship of God are set to music, because the music impresses the thought. Hugh Reginald Haweis, in "Music and Morals," says:

As emotion exists independently of Thought, so also does Music. But Music may be appropriately wedded to Thought. It is a mistake to suppose that the music itself always gains by being associated with words, or definite ideas of any sort. The words often gain a good deal, but the music is just as good without them. I do not mean to deny that images and thoughts are capable of exciting the deepest emotions, but they are inadequate to express the emotions they excite. Music is more adequate, and hence will often seize an emotion that may have been excited by an image, and partially expressed by words—will deepen its expression, and, by so doing, will excite a still deeper emotion. That is how words gain by being set to music.—*Music and Morals,* p. 35.

Hence, by means of the music ordained for Christian worship, the thought in the teaching and admonition is impressed and the worshipers are edified.

CHAPTER IX.

Psallo in the Septuagint with the Bearing of the Revised Version on the Question.

It is the purpose in this chapter to examine the argument based on the Septuagint use of *psallo*, and to note the bearing of the Revised Version on the issue. We choose to consider the latter first in order.

It will be readily admitted by all candid and well-informed persons that, in the British and American Revision of the Authorized Version of the Holy Scriptures, is represented the world's ripest scholarship. Many persons, otherwise intelligent and well informed, are not aware of the magnitude of the task which was undertaken by these masters of language and literature, and they are, therefore, without any adequate conception or just appreciation of the character and degree of learning necessary for the work.

As the scholarship represented in this immense work has an indirect but vital and important bearing upon the leading question discussed in this volume, I invite the reader's attention to some interesting facts connected with it before considering the argument based on the Septuagint use of *psallo*.

Even the half dozen men with whom the great enterprise originated about forty years ago, together with the thirty-nine scholars invited by the Convocation of Canterbury to assist in the work, constituted a company of men whose scholarship and varied learning were sufficient to command the respect and admiration of the literary world; but when this number was subsequently augmented by another list of names with equally brilliant attainments, which brought the whole number of Revisers to sixty-seven on the British side, and which has since been known as the English Company of Revisers, there was a body of men which, for broad and varied learning in the field of Biblical research, was perhaps seldom ever equaled and never surpassed.

But this is not all. Soon after the work of forming the English Company was well under way, its promoters decided to invite the coöperation of certain eminent American scholars; and, accordingly, there were appointed in this country two Companies corresponding to the two English Companies,—one for the Old Testament and the other for the New, the late William Henry Green, of Princeton, Chairman of the former, and the late Theodore D. Woolsey, Ex-President of Yale University, Chairman of the latter. In all, there were, on the British side, thirty-seven members of the Old Testament Company, and thirty of the New Testament Company; and on the American side, fifteen in the Old Testament Company, and nineteen in the New Testament

Company, making a grand total, including all on both sides of the Atlantic, of one hundred and one scholars. Vacancies caused by death or resignation during the fourteen years spent on the work were filled by the appointment of other eminent scholars of like attainments.

Now, the bearing of the course pursued in the Revision by this distinguished array of scholars on the issue now before us, is significant and far-reaching. Without a single exception, they all belonged to religious bodies which use instrumental music in the worship, and if they could consistently have given the practice any support in their revision of the old version, or in making a new translation of any particular passages, they would most assuredly have done so. Popular sentiment and popular practice were both in favor of it; and if the word *psallo* bore any meaning in New Testament times favorable to the practice, we may rest assured that they would have taken advantage of the fact.

On precisely the same principle, all the King James Translators and the great majority of the Revisers, belonging to religious bodies which practice pouring and sprinkling for baptism, would in both cases have translated the term *baptizo* in a way to support their practice if their scholarship had permitted them to do so. They knew that the word had no such meaning; and hence, as they *could not* correctly translate it so as to support their practice, they *would not* translate it so as to condemn it, and so they decided merely to Anglicize it, and did not translate it at all.

But the case concerning the meaning of *psallo* is even stronger than that concerning the meaning of *baptizo*. Not simply a majority of the religious bodies represented by the Revisers, but all of them use instrumental music in the worship. Hence, so far as theological reasons were concerned, everything was in favor of rendering *psallo* so as to uphold the practice, and no conceivable consideration would have kept them from doing so, if it could have been done with any show of consistency. But, after spending fourteen years of arduous labor on the Old and New Testaments before bringing their task to completion, what is their verdict? What do these distinguished scholars say is the meaning of *psallo* in the New Testament? Did they venture to say that the word, in any instance, means to play an instrument of music? They did not. In not a solitary instance of the use of this word by any writer of the New Testament do they tell us it has such a meaning. Why is this? Why did they not tell us, in substance, that it means "to play a stringed instrument with the fingers?" For the support of such a rendering, they could have appealed to the great lexicon of Liddell and Scott—the very highest extant authority in classic Greek—for they specifically give this, in so many words, as one of the meanings of the term.* Can any thoughtful person fail to see

---

*See Chapter VII. for facts accounting for their testimony touching its New Testament meaning.

that, in such a case, with every other consideration overwhelmingly in favor of such a rendering, nothing would ever have kept the Revisers from it except their unquestioned knowledge of the meaning of *psallo* in the New Testament period? No honest and intelligent witness will testify in court against his own interests and desires, except by the inexorable demands of truth and consistency.

Now, so far were these scholars from translating the word as meaning to play an instrument, or even by any other term directly or indirectly favoring such a meaning, they translate it, as the King James Translators had done, in all of its five occurrences, with one exception, by the verb *to sing*. The one exception is Eph. 5: 19 where they translate it, "making melody," but the context of the passage, as the Revisers rightly recognize, defines the "melody" to be "in" or "with the heart," which is simply a figurative expression for *singing*. This passage furnishes a fine illustration of the antithesis between the original classic use of *psallo*, and the use which it had come to have before the opening of the New Testament period. The Greek participial clause: "Ψάλλοντες ἐν τῇ καρδίᾳ ὑμῶν τῷ Κυρίῳ," correctly rendered in the Revised Version, "*making melody with your heart to the Lord*," institutes a vivid contrast and antithesis between the melody made during the classic period by literally striking the chords of a musical instrument, and that made during the later period by figuratively striking the chords of the hu-

89

man heart. In the language of the lamented Robert Milligan, perhaps the equal in scholarship of any man of his day and country: "The antithesis here is certainly very marked, and seems to be intentional and significant."—*Scheme of Redemption,* p. 386.

We conclude that, so far as the work of the Revisers is concerned, the English-speaking world, with the Revised New Testament as their guide, would never once think of instrumental music in the worship of a church of Christ.

But we are here informed that, notwithstanding the conclusion to which we are led by the brilliant array of scholarship represented by the Canterbury Revisers, we are, nevertheless, confronted with the fact that the Septuagint—the Greek version of the Old Testament made at Alexandria—which represents another array of scholarship, uses the term *psallo* as a translation of certain Hebrew words which all scholars admit mean to play an instrument of music, and that, therefore, *psallo* must mean the same thing. We shall now undertake to expose the fallacy which lurks in this argument, and to show that those who make it not only gain nothing, but lose much, when they attempt to trace *psallo* by the circuitous route that leads through the Greek of the Septuagint back to the original Hebrew.

We introduce this phase of the subject with a quotation from Professor Clinton Lockhart, of Christian University. Answering the question, "Can you tell me the passages in the Septuagint where *psallo* occurs, and the Hebrew of which it is a translation, and the definition of the same?" he makes the following reply:

In the following passages *psallo* is a translation of *zamar,* which means to play an instrument or to sing with instrumental accompaniment: Jud. 5: 3; 2 Sam. 22: 50; Psa. 7: 17; 9: 2, 11; 18: 49; 21: 13; 27: 6; 30: 4, 12; 33: 2; 47: 6 (four times), 7; 57: 8, 9; 59: 17; 61: 8; 66: 2, 4 (twice); 68: 4, 32; 71: 22, 23 (tells how); 75: 9; 98: 4, 5; 101: 1; 104: 33; 108: 1, 2; 105: 2; 135: 3; 138: 1; 144: 9; 146: 2; 147: 7; 149: 3; 92: 1. *To play* is a translation of *nagan,* which means to strike strings, to play on an instrument, but does not mean to sing. (1 Sam. 16: 16, 17, 23; 19: 9; 2 Ki. 3: 15; Psa. 33: 3—second verb.)

Then, commenting on certain Hebrew words, he further says:

Shir everywhere means simply to sing, to chant. The noun from *shir* and *shirah* means a song, a hymn. The finite verb meaning simply to sing is nowhere translated *psallo,* but the participle once (Psa. 68: 25) is so translated. *Zamar,* found only in the piel form, *zimmēr,* means to touch the chords of an instrument, to play, to sing with an instrument, and, when done in honor of some person, to celebrate."— *Stark-Warlick Debate,* p. 98.

Thus, he tells us that *zamar* means "to sing with instrumental accompaniment," and that "to play is a translation of *nagan,* which means to strike strings, to play on an instrument, but does not mean to sing," and we accept both of these statements as correct. He then says: "*Shir* everywhere means simply to sing, to chant," and we accept this statement also as correct. Hence, according to these statements and admissions, we have the fact that *nagan* always means to play an instrument, but never means to sing; that *zamar* means to sing, though it also means to sing with instrumental accompaniment; and that *shir* always means simply to sing, and never means to play an instrument.

We now state, as recognized by Professor Lockhart, that *psallo* appears in the Septuagint as a translation of all of these words—*nagan, zamar,* and *shir:* once for *shir;* a few times for *nagan;* and, as Thayer's lexicon says, "much oftener for *zamar.*"

It is, therefore, pertinent to ask, if *nagan* always means to play on an instrument, and never means to sing, and *zamar,* though meaning to sing with instrumental accompaniment, yet means also simply to sing or to sing praises—being rendered in this last sense almost uniformly in the Revised Version—and *shir* means nothing but to sing, how can *psallo* stand in the Septuagint as the representative of all these words? The answer is ready at hand. It is simply because of the fact, abundantly shown elsewhere in this work, that *psallo,* for several centuries before the beginning of the Christian era, was undergoing a process of change in meaning; and the Septuagint version, which was made about two hundred years before Christ, was therefore made while this process was going on. We have already seen, from the standard Greek lexicons, that all the stages of meaning through which the word passed are distinctly recognized and put down by the authors of these lexicons. Summed up by Leonard F. Bittle, as quoted elsewhere in this work, they are as follows:

In its primary sense, *psallo* had no reference to music at all, but meant merely to touch or twitch or pull; then it was used to denote the drawing of the bowstring in shooting arrows; afterwards it was restricted to making music on a harp by touching its strings; then it was applied to singing with the accompaniment of harp-music; finally it was used to denote singing psalms without any instrument save the organs of speech. In this last and latest sense it is used exclusively in the New Testament.

The reader will please note carefully, as well stated in the foregoing extract, the different stages of meaning which the word had at different times.

Now, while it is a fact that, out of the fifteen occurrences of *nagan* in the Hebrew Bible, *psallo* is given as its representative in the Septuagint in about ten of them, it is also a fact that, out of the forty-seven occurrences of *zamar, psallo* is given as its representative in the great majority of them, and one time it is given as the representative of *shir,* which never means anything but to sing. *Psallo* had not lost all of its classical meaning when the Septuagint was made, and this fact will account for its use a few times to represent *nagan;* but it is also a fact that the particular Hebrew verb (*zamar*), for which *psallo* is used oftener in the Septuagint than for any other Hebrew word, not only means to sing without any instrumental accompaniment at all, but this meaning was so well established that frequently when it was used in connection with instrumental accompaniment a separate word was used to denote the instrument both in the Hebrew Bible and in the Septuagint. This is true in Psa. 33: 2; 98: 5; 147: 7; 149: 3.

The author freely concedes that *zamar* meant to play an instrument of music, just as *psallo* in classic Greek meant the same thing; but, that its prevailing idea in the Hebrew Bible is "to sing" or "to sing praises," is abundantly recognized in the lexicons as well as in the Revised Version. We here note what the Hebrew lexicons say of this word:

1. Fuerst's Hebrew and Chaldee Lexicon defines it thus:

1. *To buzz, to hum,* i. e. *to sing.* 2. Figuratively, *to sing with the accompaniment of an instrument,* i. e. *to play;* then *to praise, to celebrate, to dance, to leap,* as far as song was the main thought in the act. Piel 1. *to sing,* used of the voice, along with *shir,* Psa. 27: 6; 57: 8; 105: 2 and *ranan* Psa. 98: 4 with which it is identical; Septuagint *humnein.* Specifically *to celebrate,* i. e. to glorify one in song, *to praise, to extol,* particularly God. 2. *to play,* with be* of the instrument, as Psa. 33: 2; 98: 5; 149: 3, properly to accompany the song with instruments, as was

---

*The Hebrew Inseparable Preposition for " in " or " with."

customary in ancient times; Septuagint *psallein* (properly to finger, to touch).

2. GESENIUS' Hebrew and English Lexicon says:

To touch or *strike* the chords of an instrument, *to play,* Greek *psallein;* and hence *to sing, to chant,* as accompanying an instrument. With dative of person *to* or *in honor of* whom, that is, *to celebrate.* Sometimes with BE of instrument.

Note that, after he gives "Greek *psallein*" as its equivalent, he adds: "and hence *to sing,* to *chant,*" showing clearly the conception which this eminent Hebraist had of the meaning which *psallo* was then coming to have.

3. The recent Hebrew and English Lexicon of BROWN, DRIVER, and BRIGGS—a work exhibiting painstaking and extended research—says:

Make music in praise of God—*make music, melody;*—1. of *singing* to God. 2. of playing musical instruments.

Of the noun, *zimrah,* the same authority says:

Melody, song, in praise of—1. of instrumental music. 2. of singing.

4. PARKHURST'S Hebrew and English Lexicon says:

To sing, or *utter harmoniously,* as a psalm or the like, pruned,* as it were, *from all irregular and discordant sounds.*

---

*Alluding to the root-meaning of *zamar,* to "prune" or "cut off."

5. BAGSTER's Hebrew-English Lexicon says:

Cut, prune, Piel, *he sang,* with BE; *celebrated the praises of,* with LE.*

In recognition of the prevailing meaning thus vouched for by the lexicons, the Revised Version, as also to some extent the King James Version, renders *zamar* simply to *"sing praises."* The following passages may be consulted in illustration: Jud. 5: 3; 2 Sam. 22: 50; Psa. 7: 17; 9: 2; 27: 6; 30: 4; 47: 6; 59: 17; 61: 8; 75: 9; 101: 1. In these, and many other passages, the expressions, *"sing praise"* and *"sing praises,"* both represent zamar in the original.

We are now warranted in certain conclusions concerning the Septuagint:

1. The use of *psallo* in that version to represent different Hebrew words varying in meaning from that of playing on a musical instrument to singing with instrumental accompaniment, and then to singing without any instrument at all except the organs of speech, is in harmony with, and partly confirmatory of, the position that the word was then in process of change. It should be remembered, as before observed, that the Septuagint was made two hundred years before Christ and *psallo* had not yet altogether changed from its classical meaning, though it was even then rapidly taking on the meaning simply "to sing."

---

*The Hebrew Inseparable Preposition for " to " or " unto."

2. The fact that it was then in process of change, and that at the opening of the New Testament period two hundred years later this change had been completely effected so that it had come to mean simply *to sing,* is a complete exposure of the fallacy of resorting to the Septuagint for support for any other meaning in the New Testament. As observed in another chapter, this course with *psallo* is precisely on a par with the course of those who might assert that "silly" means to be "fortunate" or "happy," and then resort to Chaucer to prove it!

CHAPTER X.

———

Apostolic Example and Instrumental Music.

———

In the search for divine authority for instrumental music in Christian worship, its apologists sometimes attempt to find it in the example of some of the Apostles. It is claimed that inspired Apostles, and particularly Peter and John, worshiped God under Christ with instrumental music, and that, therefore, we have apostolic example for the practice in Christian worship.

Let it be cheerfully conceded, first of all, that if this claim be founded in fact—if, indeed, we have apostolic example for the practice, then all opposition to it should cease; for, if we are not to follow the leadership of inspired Apostles in our efforts to worship and serve God, then we are in hopeless confusion, and it is needless to look anywhere else for guidance.

But what are the facts about this important claim? "To the law and to the testimony," shall be our appeal. The claim in question is based upon the conduct of Peter and John as recorded in the third chapter of the book of Acts. It is alleged that, when these Apostles went into the temple at the hour of prayer, they went for the purpose of engaging in the worship as there conducted, and that they did engage in said worship; that instrumental music was used in that worship; and hence that the use of such music in Christian worship has on it the stamp of apostolic approval.

It is much easier to affirm than to prove; and we now propose to show that the foregoing string of assertions, so far as the one essential thing to be proved is concerned, are utterly without foundation in fact. Even those statements in the list which are true, (and some of them are true), have nothing whatever to do with the point at issue, have not, in fact, the remotest bearing on it, so that the case is not affected by them one way or another. It is amazing to see how even strong men, when committed to the defense of what they cannot prove, will resort to a process of reasoning which assumes or takes for granted the very thing which they have set out to prove. This effort to find support in apostolic example for instrumental music in Christian worship is a conspicuous illustration of this fact. In his debate with Brother W. W. Otey in 1908, Brother J. B. Briney stated the case as follows:

Not only before the day of Pentecost, but afterwards Peter and John were going up into the Temple at the ninth hour of the day, and there were these instruments of music, and that these men went up there to participate in those devotions where these instruments were being used, it seems to me, does not admit of reasonable doubt, and yet, notwithstanding the fact that the Savior was there in his lifetime, and notwithstanding the fact that the Apostles frequented that Temple and participated in those thanks and adoration and praise, yet not one line or one word or one sentence ever fell from Apostle, Prophet or Christ in condemnation of that practice.—*Otey-Briney Debate,* p. 44.

We desire now to analyze and examine these statements, and especially their logical bearing upon the point in dispute. They are four in number, as follows: (1). "Peter and John were going up into the Temple at the ninth hour of the day." (2). "There were these instruments of music." (3). "That these men went up there to participate in those devotions where these instruments were being used, it seems to me, does not admit of reasonable doubt." (4). "Notwithstanding the fact that the Apostles frequented that Temple, and participated in those thanks and adoration and praise, yet not one line or one word or one sentence ever fell from Apostle, Prophet or Christ in condemnation of that practice."

Now, suppose "Peter and John were going up into the Temple at the ninth hour;" and suppose it is true that "there were these instruments of music;" and suppose, furthermore, that "not one line or one word or one sentence ever fell from Apostle, Prophet or Christ in condemnation of that practice,"—suppose all this is true, still we are confronted with the stubborn fact that, so far as the one point here at issue is concerned, everything depends upon whether the thing assumed in number 3 is true or false. But the unvarnished fact here is that what is assumed in number 3 is nothing more nor less than a bald and groundless assumption with not one word, fact, or intimation in the entire record that proves it. The very thing to be proved is coolly assumed and reasoned on as a settled fact. The author of the statement himself approaches it rather cautiously. He only says "it seems to" him that Peter and John "went up there to participate in those devotions where these instruments were being used;" but where is the proof of it? And why should it "seem" so in the absence of proof? The very utmost that can here be claimed is that the point assumed is a mere inference, but by no means a necessary inference. There is not one word in the whole record that says they were going into the Temple for that purpose, and not a single fact from which it is a necessary inference. Moreover, not only is all this true, but there are clear and indisputable facts in the record which show conclusively that Peter and John went into the Temple for a very different purpose. We now appeal to the record for a verification of this point, and we begin with the third chapter of Acts.

1. It is clearly stated in the record that Peter and John went up into the Temple at the hour of prayer, 3: 1. There is, therefore, no room for dispute on this point.

2. But what did they go for? Everything hinges here. Now, if there could have been no other purpose in going into the Temple at that hour except "to participate in those devotions," then the fact of their going thither at that hour would, of course, be proof of the point in dispute; but this is not only not true, but the record plainly and specifically states a different purpose for which the Apostles went into the Temple. That this purpose may be clearly seen, we will now examine the facts in detail.

(1). Beginning with the third chapter of Acts, we find, first of all, that, as "Peter and John were going up into the Temple," they found the lame man whom the people "laid daily at the door of the Temple which is called Beautiful, to ask alms of them that entered into the Temple," vv. 1, 2.

(2). This lame man "seeing Peter and John about to go into the Temple, asked to receive an alms," v. 3.

(3). Then followed the miracle of healing. The Apostle said: "Silver and gold have I none; but what I have, that give I thee. In the name of Jesus Christ of Nazareth, walk," v. 6.

(4). Being immediately healed, the lame man "stood, and began to walk; and he entered with them into the Temple, walking, and leaping, and praising God," v. 8.

(5). When the people saw what was done, "they were filled with wonder and amazement at that which had happened unto him," and they all "ran together unto them in the porch that is called Solomon's," vv. 10, 11.

(6). At this juncture Peter, promptly seizing the opportunity, delivered a strong and convincing sermon, proclaiming the death, burial, and resurrection of Jesus of Nazareth, and thus set forth the new order of worship and service to God which had come to supersede the service belonging to the Temple, vv. 12-26.

(7). This at once produced a clash between Peter and John on the one hand, and the Temple authorities on the other, the latter "being sore troubled because they taught the people, and proclaimed in Jesus the resurrection from the dead;" and the extent to which the devotees of the Temple worship were stirred up is seen in the fact that they at once had Peter and John arrested and put in prison, 4: 1-3.

(8). The next important fact in Luke's record of these interesting proceedings is his statement of the effect of Peter's sermon upon the people, when he says: "Many of them that heard the word believed; and the number of the men came to be about five thousand," v. 4.

(9). Following Luke in his continuous narrative of apostolic proceedings in and about the Temple, he says that "by the hands of the Apostles were many signs and wonders wrought among the people; and they were all with one accord in Solomon's porch. But of the rest durst no man join himself to them; howbeit the people magnified them; and believers were the more added to the Lord, multitudes both of men and women," 5: 12-14.

(10). We now reach the climax of proof touching the purpose for which the Apostles went into the temple, when we are informed by Luke that, as the result of their labors thus far in the Temple, "the high priest rose up, and all they that were with him (which is the sect of the Sadducees), and they were filled with jealousy, and laid hands on the Apostles, and put them in public ward," whereupon "an angel of the Lord by night opened the prison doors, and brought them out and said, Go ye, and stand and speak in the Temple to the people all the words of this Life; and when they heard this, they entered into the Temple about daybreak, and taught." On the following day, thinking their prisoners were secure within the prison, "the high priest came, and they that were with him, and called the council together, and all the senate of the children of Israel, and sent to the prison-house to have them brought. But the officers that came found them not in the prison; and they returned, and told, saying, The prison-house we found shut in all safety, and the keepers standing at the doors; but when we had opened, we found no man within." The captain of the Temple and the chief priests were dumfounded at this unexpected turn in the current of events, and while they were perplexed over the situation, "there came one and told them, Behold, the men whom ye put in the prison are in the Temple standing and teaching the people," vv. 17-25. Finally, when they were again arrested and brought before the council for trial, the high priest said: "We strictly charged you not to teach in this name; and behold, ye have filled Jerusalem with your teaching, and intend to bring this man's blood upon us," to which the resolute Apostles replied: "We must obey God rather than men;" and after being beaten by the council and charged "not to speak in the name of Jesus," Luke informs us that they "departed from the presence of the council, rejoicing that they were counted worthy to suffer dishonor for the Name." He then adds the significant statement that "every day, in the Temple and at home, they ceased not to teach and to preach Jesus as the Christ," vv. 27-42.

Now, in the light of this array of facts, the purpose for which the Apostles went into the Temple is so clearly set forth that it amounts to nothing short of a demonstration. The angel of the Lord said: "Go ye, and stand and speak in the Temple to the people all the words of this Life." Luke tells us that they promptly entered into the Temple "and taught." An unnamed person came and reported to the council: "Behold, the men whom ye put in the prison are in the Temple standing and teaching the people." On the very occasion when Peter and John went into the Temple at the hour of prayer, while the object of their going is not stated by Luke in immediate connection with his statement of the fact that they went into the Temple, yet a little further on in his narrative he gives it by giving what they did in the Temple. He not only informs us

105

that they preached to the people there assembled,
but he gives substantially a part of the powerful
and effective sermon delivered by Peter on the occasion by which he converted many persons to the
Christian faith. And finally, to put the matter beyond all doubt and disputation, Luke states the fact
that "every day, in the Temple and at home, they
ceased not to teach and to preach Jesus as the
Christ."

Now, not only do we have all this plainly in the
record, but there is not one word that says they
"went up there to participate in those devotions."
Yea, more; not only is there not a word in the record that says they went there to engage in the Temple worship, but there is not a word that says they
went there to worship at all. The record specifically
gives a different purpose which led them into the
Temple, namely, to introduce the new faith and the
new order of worship under Christ. Moreover, as
a matter of fact, this new faith and the new order of
worship, which we have now seen they went into the
Temple to introduce, would completely change and
supersede "those devotions" belonging to the Temple service, except in so far as they contained something which the Lord incorporated in the new order. The record distinctly shows that they went
there to teach the word of God, to preach the new
faith and establish the new order of worship, and
they went to the Temple because they could there
find the people many of whom would be ready and

willing to hear their message, just as, on precisely the same principle, they subsequently went into the synagogues of the Jews throughout the Roman empire to preach the same new faith and establish the same new order of worship under Christ.

We are, therefore, irresistibly led to the conclusion that whoever, in order to find support for instrumental music in Christian worship, appeals to the fact that the Apostles went into the Jewish Temple where such music was used in the Jewish worship, appeals to a record that does not contain a single statement, fact, or word in support of the practice.

CHAPTER XI.

The Harps and Harpers of Revelation.

Even if "the four living creatures and the four and twenty elders" who "fell down before the Lamb" with the "one hundred and forty-four thousand standing on mount Zion," and the "victorious" hosts "standing by the sea of glass" in the vision of John on Patmos, did use not only harps, but all other kinds of musical instruments in the praise of God, it would not logically follow, as the thoughtful and well informed will admit, that therefore such instruments may be used by Christians in the worship of God here on earth, any more than it would follow, from the fact that such instruments were used in the Jewish worship, that therefore they may be used in Christian worship; and it is no part of my purpose here to attempt to defend a point which is so self-evident and so well established.

But, there is another and radically different use made in modern times of these "harpers harping with their harps," to which I invite attention, and which it is the purpose here to examine with care. The terms to be examined are contained in the following passages: "And when he had taken the book, the four living creatures and the four and twenty elders fell down before the Lamb, having each one a harp, and golden bowls full of incense, which are the prayers of the saints. And they sing a new song, saying, Worthy art thou to take the book, and to open the seals thereof; for thou wast slain, and didst purchase unto God with thy blood men of every tribe, and tongue, and people, and nation," Rev. 5: 8, 9. "And I saw, and behold, the Lamb standing on the mount Zion, and with him a hundred and forty and four thousand, having his name, and the name of his Father, written on their foreheads. And I heard a voice from heaven, as the voice of many waters, and as the voice of a great thunder; and the voice which I heard was as the voice of harpers harping with their harps; and they sing as it were a new song before the throne, and before the four living creatures and the elders; and no man could learn the song save the hundred and forty and four thousand, even they that had been purchased out of the earth," Rev. 14: 1-3. "And I saw as it were a sea of glass mingled with fire; and them that come off victorious from the beast, and from his image, and from the number of his name, standing by the sea of glass, having harps of God. And they sing the song of Moses the servant of God, and the song of the Lamb," Rev. 15: 2, 3.

Now, it is alleged that, while the Greek word *ode* (ᾠδή), which is the word used in Eph. 5: 19 and Col. 3: 16 and translated "song," and in the verb form "to sing," does not convey, in and of itself, the idea of instrumental music, yet when we go to these passages just cited in Revelation where the same word is used, we find that when they "sang the *ode*," they used harps, and that therefore, when we sing the *ode*, as we are authorized in Eph. 5: 19 and Col. 3: 16 to do, we also may use harps, or other instruments. That the logic of this position may be seen as set forth by those who avow it, we quote here the following comment on these passages by Brother J. B. Briney in the Otey-Briney debate:

How are they singing this ode? How are they rendering this song? They are rendering it in connection with harps, that is, in connection with instruments of music. Now, says the Apostle, sing the ode, and I turn over here and I find out that those who sang the ode did it in connection with the harp and other instruments of music, and thus God's approval rests upon it. * * * There it is, my friends, singing the song of Moses, because Moses was the type of Christ, singing the song of the Lamb, who was Christ, and they did that in connection with the use of harps and other instruments of music. Now, if we are authorized to sing psalms, and we find out that those who sang the psalms did so in connection with instruments of music, and if we are admonished to sing the ode, and we find out that those who sang the ode did it in connection with instruments of music, and that God approved it, who shall say nay?—*pp*. 47, 48.

We now propose a respectful examination of this logic together with the facts in the case, and then we may be better prepared to say "who shall say nay."

1. Answering the questions, "How are they singing this ode? How are they rendering this song?" the author of this logic says: "They are rendering it in connection with harps." Well, what if they are? What if they are rendering it in connection with harps and every other kind of musical instrument that was ever made? They are not a church of Jesus Christ. They are not an assembly of Christians worshiping God here on earth during the Christian dispensation; and hence nothing that they are doing, that is, simply because they are doing it, can be properly quoted as an example governing the worship of such an assembly of Christians. Who, then, are these persons mentioned in Revelation, and where are they? John tells us that they are "before the throne and before the Lamb, arrayed in white robes, and palms in their hands;" that "the four living creatures and the four and twenty elders" with "many angels round about the throne" are among them; that they have "come out of the great tribulation" having "washed their robes and made them white in the blood of the Lamb;" and that "they shall hunger no more, neither thirst any more; neither shall the sun strike upon them, nor any heat; for the Lamb that is in the midst of the throne shall be their Shepherd, and shall guide them unto fountains of waters of life; and God shall wipe away every tear from their eyes."

These are some of the terms in which John introduces us to this celestial company. The idea of quoting what they are doing and setting it forth as an example governing the worship of a church of Christ here on earth, is certainly wide of the mark. Be it said, once for all, that, on the hypothesis that there is a literal material "sea of glass mingled with fire," and that these are literal material harps, if God sees proper to have such instruments of music in His worship in heaven, nobody, of course, should object to it, and no loyal child of God would object to it. Neither would such a child of God object to it in His worship here on earth, if He should see proper to have it there.

2. The author of the logic now under review, referring to these "harpers harping with their harps" in heaven, says: "Thus God's approval rests upon it." Certainly "God's approval rests upon it" *in that worship,* precisely as, at the same time and in *the same worship,* "God's approval" rested upon "golden bowls full of incense," "a golden censer," and "the golden altar which was before the throne" where "the smoke of the incense, with the prayers of the saints, went up before God." Hence, according to the logic now under examination, a church of Jesus Christ is divinely authorized to have "golden bowls full of incense," "a golden censer," and a "golden altar," to set them up in the place of worship, and there burn incense on the golden altar in the worship of God. If not, why not? If any stickler for divine authority should call in question the use of golden bowls full of incense, a golden censer,

a golden altar, and the burning of incense in the worship of God to-day, the author of this logic could promptly say: "There it is, my friends, singing the song of Moses, because Moses was the type of Christ, singing the song of the Lamb, who was Christ, and they did that in connection with the use of" GOLDEN BOWLS, A GOLDEN CENSER, A GOLDEN ALTAR, AND THE BURNING OF INCENSE, "and if we are admonished to sing the ode, and we find out that those who sang the ode did it in connection with" GOLDEN BOWLS, A GOLDEN CENSER, A GOLDEN ALTAR, AND THE BURNING OF INCENSE, "and that God approved it, who shall say nay?" From the premises laid down, this conclusion inevitably follows, and there is no escape from it.

3. We will now examine the Greek word ᾠδή (*ode*), which is the word used in connection with what is related of the harps and harpers in Revelation. It is alleged, as we saw in the foregoing comment, that because harpers harping with their harps are mentioned in Revelation in connection with those who sang the ode in that heavenly worship, therefore, when we sing the ode in Christian worship here on the earth, which the Scriptures tell us to do, we may harp with harps, or use other instruments of music. The assumption is that the word "*ode*" carries with it the idea of the harp or other such instrument, and that the case of the harpers in Revelation shows us how to "render the ode," namely, by accompanying it with harps or other such instruments of music.

Now, this is purely a groundless assumption, in

support of which there is not a solitary fact in Revelation or elsewhere in the Scriptures, nor anything in the definition of the word. We can settle this point by appealing to the Greek scholars who have defined the word for us.

(1). Thayer defines ᾠδή, the noun, as follows: "*a song, lay, ode;* in the Scriptures a song in praise of God or Christ." He defines ᾄδω, which is the same word in the verb form, as follows: "*to sing, chant.*"

(2). Sophocles defines ᾠδή: "*ode, song.*" He defines the verb simply: "*to sing.*"

(3). Robinson: "*ᾠδή an ode, song,* e. g. in praise of God;" the verb: "*to sing,* with Dative of person *to sing to* any one, in his praise and honor."

(4). Liddell and Scott: "*ᾠδή a song, lay, ode; song, singing.*" The verb: "*to sing;* hence, all kinds of vocal sounds, *to crow,* as cocks, *twitter* as swallows, *hoot* as owls, *croak* as frogs, etc.; also of other sounds, *to twang,* of the bowstring; *to whistle,* of the wind through a tree; *to ring,* of a stone when struck; *to sing to* one; *to sing, chant.*"

It is needless to quote other authorities. These are sufficient to show, beyond all successful contradiction, that this term, in the noun form in the Scriptures, always means simply *a song,* an *ode,* and in the verb form, *to sing, to chant.* It has no other meaning, conveys no other idea. The definitions given by these lexicons simply exhaust the word of all the meaning it has in the word of God, and there can be no other meaning in connection with it without using additional words to convey that meaning. It is true that in connection with the use of this word in Revelation, we find other ideas, namely, harps and harping, but it is also true that in each and every case, there is an additional and different word to convey the additional idea. If the word κιθάρα (*kithara*), meaning a harp, or some other word with that meaning, had not been used, no such idea as "harp" would be in the passage. It would never have been dreamed of from the mere use of the word ᾠδή (*ode*); and if the word κιθαρῳδός (*kitharodos*), meaning a harper, had not been used, the idea of "harper" would not be in the passage, nor would it be even remotely suggested by the word ᾠδή; and, in like manner, if the word κιθαρίζω (*kitharizo*), or its equivalent, had not been used in the passage, the idea of harping would not have been thought of, except as suggested by the words meaning "harp" and "harper." The term ᾠδή (*ode*) suggests no such idea.

Now, what are the facts about the use of this word (ᾠδή, *ode*), and the harps and harpers mentioned in the book of Revelation? Nothing more nor less than simply this, namely, the harpers and the harping with the words which signify them, and the singers and the singing with the words which signify them, are merely found in use at the same time and place and in the same worship; but certainly it does not follow from this that the one implies the other, or that where we may find the one to be authorized by the Lord, the other is also so authorized. Of

115

course both may be so authorized, but we may never rightly so conclude unless both are specified. The one does not involve or imply the other. It so happens that both are found to be used in the instance of worship which the book of Revelation mentions as taking place after the close of the Christian dispensation, just as both are found to have been in use in the Jewish worship before the Christian dispensation began; *but we do not find both in use by divine authority during the Christian dispensation;* and this is precisely the point on which the whole issue turns. During this dispensation, the Lord has abundantly authorized His children to sing the ode in His worship, but He has nowhere authorized them to play the *kithara* in that worship. We find odes, and the singing of odes, but no *kithara*, nor the playing of the *kithara*. When the Lord says *ode*, He does not mean *kithara;* and, according to the definition of these terms by lexical scholarship, *ode* never implies *kithara*. As we have already seen, *kithara* (harp) and *ode* may be found together in the same worship, but always because each, independently of the other, is specifically named and thus authorized to be there, and never because either involves or implies the other. Hence, to argue that, because we find both at a given time in a given worship, we may, therefore, have both at any other time in any other worship when and where only one of them is specified, is, to say the least of it, a figment, pure and simple, without a single fact in either philology or the Bible

116

to sustain it. When the advocates of a cause are forced to resort to such reasoning in order to find a shadow of support for it, simply because they cannot resort to anything better, there is good ground for the presumption that there is, in reality, nothing to sustain it. Hence, with due consideration for the views and feelings of those who have hitherto been led to think otherwise, I respectfully add that this, it seems to me, is the only rational conclusion that can be reached in regard to this modern claim concerning the harps and harpers of Revelation.

CHAPTER XII.

The Claim Concerning Clement and Ambrose.

Among the various resorts of modern apologists for instrumental music in the worship, is the claim that it was so used in the fourth century by the celebrated Ambrose of Milan, and even as early as the close of the second century by Clement of Alexandria. This claim is put forth in the effort to break, or at least modify, the force of the position that instrumental music was never used in Christian worship till about the sixth or the seventh century, and that there was no general use of it till several hundred years after that time.

Be it remembered, first of all, that even were this claim established by clear and indisputable facts, it would prove nothing at all, so far as divine authority is concerned, which is the point at issue. It would only prove that this innovation was introduced at an earlier date than is usually assigned to it; only this, and nothing more. In fact, so far as the real issue is concerned, whether it was introduced by Ambrose in the fourth century or by Clement in the second century; or, indeed, whether it was introduced in the first century or the twentieth century, makes no difference whatever in principle, so long as it remains a fact that it was introduced after the days of Inspiration. If the practice is shown to be without divine authority, then the only point which its opponents are under logical obligation to prove is fully established, no matter when nor by whom it was introduced.

But, the use which has been made of this claim both in books and in periodical literature in recent years has led the present author to make a careful examination of the subject of music as treated in the literature of the early centuries; and he has been unable to find anything whatever which can be relied on as proof that either Ambrose or Clement ever said or did anything that justifies the claim in question. In fact, there is ground for serious doubt, as we shall see, whether Clement ever used the language which has been attributed to him, and the writers who have made the claim concerning Ambrose have failed, as far as we have been able to see, to produce any proof of their claim.

It is the purpose in the present chapter, to present the facts in the case, and then submit the question to the candid decision of the reader.

1. The Claim as to Ambrose.

This celebrated church "father" and Bishop of the cathedral church of Milan, who was born A.D. 340, and died A.D. 397, was a great musician, the so-called "Ambrosian chant" being named in his honor. Now, it is not only claimed that he used instrumental music in the worship, but the claim is sometimes accompanied with the assumption that its use, even at that early period, was looked upon as a mere matter of course and met with no opposition. While, of course, the mere fact that a given fact is not mentioned by reliable historians in connection with Ambrose is not proof that he did not teach it, still it creates a presumption in favor of the position that he did not, and the burden of proof rests upon those who set up the claim that he did. Now, in the present case, we merely contend that the evidence that he did so teach is not conclusive.

We now invite attention to the facts in the case. Sir John Hawkins, an author whom we have quoted elsewhere in this work, and who lived no farther back than the eighteenth century, is the authority that is relied on as proof of the aforesaid claim. We already have his admission (See Chap. XIV., page 151 of this work) that in the primitive church, when the worship was under the supervision and guidance of inspired men, only vocal music was used in the praise of God. Remember, too, as just stated, that Sir John Hawkins lived no farther back than the eighteenth century. To be exact, he was born in London, England, and lived from 1719 to 1789 after the use of instrumental music in the worship, with many other perversions of the ancient order, had become general. Moreover, he threw himself, with all the strength he could command, on the side of those favoring the practice, and he would not likely omit, from his general history of music, any available proof that would, in his judgment, sustain that side of the question; yet the following is the sum of his testimony on this point:

> Though it is uncontroverted that Vitalianus introduced the organ into the service of the Romish church, yet the use of instruments in churches was much earlier; for we are told that St. Ambrose joined instruments of music with the public service in the cathedral church of Milan, which example of his was so approved of, that by degrees it became the general practice of other churches, and has since obtained in almost all the Christian world besides. Nay, the antiquity of instrumental church music is still higher, if we may credit the testimony of Justin Martyr and Eusebius, the latter of whom lived fifty, and the former two hundred years before the time of St. Ambrose.—*General History of Music, Vol. I.,* p. 147.

But, "we are told" *by whom?* Not a word of proof is adduced. So far as the author has been able to ascertain, not a single quotation is made. We simply have the mere and unsupported statement of Sir John Hawkins who, though he no doubt made the statement honestly, nevertheless had no record, it seems, to which he could appeal as proof of his assertion. Moreover, when he adds that "the antiquity of" this practice "is still higher, if we may credit the testimony of Justin Martyr and Eusebius," why did he not quote their "testimony" to that effect, if they left any such testimony on record?

Since reading this assertion from Sir John Hawkins in his General History of Music, and examining every place in that large work in which, as it appears to us, he would likely quote such testimony from these authors, and failing to find a single quotation from them in support of his assertion, the author, simply to test its correctness and get at the facts, has taken the pains to read carefully every line of the undisputed works of Justin Martyr, his "First Apology," his "Second Apology," and his "Dialogue with Trypho the Jew," and there is not a solitary word of such "testimony" anywhere in these works. Moreover, during the same time and for the same purpose, the author has read every line of the ten Books of the Ecclesiastical History of Eusebius, the work in which he would most likely record such "testimony," if he recorded it anywhere at all, and not a line of such "testimony" does this famous work contain. We simply add that, if these men left on record a single word favoring the use of instrumental music in Christian worship, we have so far been unable to find it. But this is not all. If they left on record any such "testimony" as Sir John Hawkins intimates, then not only has the present author, but the world's historians, encyclopedists, and annotators of every class have failed to discover it. With all due respect, therefore, to his learning in the musical lore of the ages, we believe Sir John Hawkins' statement is founded in a misconception of facts.

But how shall we account for such a statement from a reputable writer? On the ground of tradition and rumor. On the hypothesis that there was such a tradition and rumor current at the time, it is easy to see how even a reputable writer, as eager to uphold instrumental music in the worship as Sir John Hawkins is known to have been, would seize the opportunity to bolster the practice by saying "we are told that St. Ambrose joined instruments of music with the public service," and in so saying he would tell the truth. Moreover, as already conceded, we cannot know, so far as the present author has seen anything to the contrary is concerned, that Ambrose did not do what is alleged of him. There were other equally gross departures from the primitive order that are known to have been adopted even before that time, such as infant baptism, and pouring and sprinkling for baptism. The McClintock and Strong Cyclopedia not only speaks, in general terms, of "heresy largely pervading the church and making rapid headway" at that very time, but it specifies "the appointment of singers as a distinct class of officers in the church" with "the consequent introduction of profane music;" and why should not instrumental music have been introduced if the carnal wishes of the people called for it? In view of such facts and tendencies at the time, it would certainly not be a matter of surprise if it were discovered that instrumental music had also been introduced. We only make the point here that the evidence thus far adduced in support of the claim is not only not conclusive, but points decidedly to the conclusion that Ambrose, at any rate, never introduced it. In fact, the McClintock and Strong Cyclopedia says:

Neither Ambrose, nor Basil, nor Chrysostom in the noble encomiums which they severally pronounced upon music, make any mention of instrumental music.—*Vol. VI.,* p. 759, *Art. Music.*

2. The Claim as to Clement.

Before presenting the body of the text from Clement containing the famous passage in dispute, we here quote the opening sentence of the passage separately for examination upon its own merits. The following is the original of this sentence: Κἂν πρὸς κιθάραν ἐθελήσῃς ἢ λύραν ᾄδειν τε καὶ ψάλλειν, μῶμος οὐκ ἔστιν. It may be rendered as follows: *And if you wish to sing and make melody to the harp and the lyre, there is no blame.*

Now, with no other light on the case except that thrown on it by these bare words themselves, we submit that it would be utterly impossible to tell whether the author of the passage meant that these instruments might be used by Christians in the worship of God, or as a mere entertainment outside of that worship. The passage itself does not specify either, while the context is decidedly in favor of the latter view. In fact, there is much in the context that is wholly out of harmony with the view that he meant the worship of God; and this position is so well sustained by the entire drift of thought in Clement that

Joseph Bingham, the eminent author of "Antiquities of the Christian Church," unhesitatingly says:

He speaks not of what was then in use in Christian churches, but of what might lawfully be used by any private Christians, if they were disposed to use it; which rather argues that instrumental music, the lute and the harp, of which he speaks, was not in use in the public churches.—*Antiq. of the Christian Church,* Vol. 2, p. 485.

But this is not all. The utterances of Clement both in the context and elsewhere are so clear, outspoken, and strong against the use of such instruments in any kind of temperate feast or assembly, that some eminent scholars are pronounced in the conviction that the passage now under review is, beyond all doubt, an interpolation. Johann Caspar Suicer, a noted Latin writer of the seventeenth century, who is the author of a Theological Thesaurus in two large quarto volumes, is very positive in his advocacy of this position. After calling attention to the place in Clement up to which the language, in his judgment, is genuine, he describes what follows as unquestionably an interpolation, using the strong and significant word, *"assumentum,"* which means one thing sewed on to another, and may be well rendered by the word "patch." He says it is "diametrically opposed to the foregoing." "Neither," he adds, "do I see with what reason they are joined to the preceding by κἄν." Then, after pointing out, in the alleged spurious passage, "a most irrelevant

question and one worthy only of a Cabalist," he
says: "It is foreign also to the piety of Clement that
the σκολιὸν instituted for drinking companies, to be
sung in the convivial feasts of the Gentiles, is said
to have been made Ἑβραικῶν κατὰ ἐικόνα ψαλμῶν. As if
he [Clement] did not know that Psalms, not 'wine
songs,' i. e. convivial songs, as the σκόλια are, although
they [i. e. Psalms] were recited at the close of the
Supper, Matt. 26: 30,—I say that so great a profana-
tion of the Psalms is most severely condemned by
God in the third [commandment] of the Decalogue
and Amos 5: 23; 6: 5, 6." Continuing his argument
further on, he adds: "In order, then, that we may
expedite the matter at last: That whole chapter of
Clement seems to be ended with Οὗτος ἡμῶν ὁ κῶμος ὁ
εὐχάριστος." Then, after citing certain incongruous
and hence evidently spurious expressions, he asks:
"By what reason would he, from the example of the
Greeks, teach that the singing is to be done to the
lyre? For in other parts everywhere he rejects [dis-
approves] that kind of voluptuous music, and the
psaltery of David he adapts [accommodates] to us
allegorically." In confirmation of this statement,
he makes certain quotations from Clement, among
which is the following from Book VI. of his "Strom-
ata:" "Superfluous music is to be rejected, because
it breaks and variously affects the mind, so that
sometimes it is indeed mournful, sometimes unchaste
and inciting to licentiousness, sometimes frenzied
and insane." Then, from Book II. of his "Pæda-

gogos:" "These instruments are to be banished from sober [temperate] feasts, which are suitable rather for beasts than for men, and for those men who are estranged from reason." After submitting a number of such statements from Clement, all of which are incongruous with the idea that he favored instrumental music in Christian worship, Suicer draws this pointed conclusion: "Nothing therefore has Clement written which would favor organs and their present-day use even the least, yea directly the contrary."—*Suicer's Thesaurus, Vol.* 2, p. 502.

In confirmation of the reasonableness of the view advocated in the foregoing,—at any rate, to show that Clement did not teach the use of instrumental music in Christian worship, we now reproduce the entire chapter in which the disputed passage or alleged interpolation occurs. It is Chapter IV. of Book II. in the work of Clement entitled "Pædagogos," or "The Instructor." We submit the English translation given in Volume II. of the "Ante-Nicene Fathers," under the editorship of Alexander Roberts and James Donaldson and styled the "American Reprint of the Edinburgh Edition." On pages 248 and 249 of this work, under the heading, "How to Conduct Ourselves at Feasts," the chapter in question appears in full, and is as follows:

Let revelry keep away from our rational entertainments, and foolish vigils, too, that revel in intemperance. For revelry is an inebriate pipe, the chain of an amatory bridge, that is, of sorrow. And let love, and intoxication, and senseless passions, be removed from our choir. Burlesque singing is the boon companion of drunkenness. A night spent over drink invites drunkenness, rouses lust, and is audacious in deeds of shame. For if people occupy their time with pipes, and psalteries, and choirs, and dances, and Egyptian clapping of hands, and such disorderly frivolities, they become quite immodest and intractable, beat on cymbals and drums, and make a noise on instruments of delusion; for plainly such a banquet, as seems to me, is a theater of drunkenness. For the apostle decrees that, "putting off the works of darkness, we should put on the armor of light, walking honestly as in the day, not spending our time in rioting and drunkenness, in chambering and wantonness." Let the pipe be resigned to the shepherds, and the flute to the superstitious who are engrossed in idolatry. For, in truth, such instruments are to be banished from the temperate banquet being more suitable to beasts than men, and the more irrational portion of mankind. For we have heard of stags being charmed by the pipe, and seduced by music into the toils when hunted by huntsmen. And when mares are being covered, a tune is played on the flute—a nuptial song, as it were. And every improper sight and sound, to speak in a word, and every shameful sensation of licentiousness—which, in truth, is privation of the sensation—must by all means be excluded; and we must be on our guard against whatever pleasure titillates eye and ear, and effeminates. For the various spells of the broken strains and plaintive numbers of the Carian muse corrupt men's morals, drawing to perturbation of mind by the licentious and mischievous art of music.

The Spirit, distinguishing from such revelry the divine service, sings, "Praise Him with the sound of trumpet;" for with sound of trumpet he shall raise the dead. "Praise Him on the psaltery;" for the tongue is the psaltery of the Lord; "And praise Him on the lyre." By the lyre is meant the mouth struck by the Spirit, as it were by a plectrum. "Praise Him with the timbrel and the dance," refers to the Church meditating on the resurrection of the dead in the resounding skin. "Praise Him on the chords and organ." Our body He calls an organ, and its nerves are the strings by which it has received harmonious tension, and when struck by the Spirit, it gives forth human voices. "Praise Him on the clashing cymbals." He calls the tongue the cymbal of the mouth, which resounds with the pulsation of the lips. Therefore He cried to humanity, "Let every breath praise the Lord," because He cares for every breathing thing which He hath made. For man is truly a pacific instrument; while other instruments, if you investigate, you will find to be warlike, inflaming to lust, or kindling up amours, or rousing wrath. In their wars, therefore, the Etruscans use the trumpet, the Arcadians the pipe, the Sicilians the pectides, the Cretans the lyre, the Lacedæmonians the flute, the Thracians the horn, the Egyptians the drum, and the Arabians the cymbal. The one instrument of peace, the word alone by which we honor God, is what we employ. We no longer employ the ancient psaltery and trumpet, and timbrel, and flute, which those expert in war and contemners of the fear of God were wont to make use of also in the choruses at their festive assemblies; that by such strains they might raise their dejected minds.

But let our genial feeling in drinking be twofold,

in accordance with the law. For, "if thou shalt love the Lord thy God" and then "thy neighbor," let its first manifestation be toward God in thanksgiving and psalmody, and the second toward our neighbor in decorous fellowship. For says the apostle, "Let the word of the Lord dwell in you richly." And this word suits and conforms himself to seasons, to persons, to places. In the present instance He is a guest with us. For the apostle adds, "Teaching and admonishing one another in all wisdom, in psalms, and hymns, and spiritual songs, singing with grace in your heart to God." And again, "Whatsoever ye do in word or deed, do all in the name of the Lord Jesus, giving thanks to God and His Father." This is our thankful revelry. And even if you wish to sing and play to the harp or lyre, there is no blame.* Thou shalt imitate the righteous Hebrew king in his thanksgiving to God. "Rejoice in the Lord, ye righteous; praise is comely to the upright," says the prophecy. "Confess to the Lord on the harp; play to Him on the psaltery of ten strings. Sing to Him a new song." And does not the ten-stringed psaltery indicate the word Jesus who is manifested by the element of the decad?† And as it is befitting, before partaking of food, that we should bless the Creator of all; so also in drinking it is suitable to praise Him on partaking of His creatures. For the psalm is a melodious and sober blessing. The apostle calls the psalm "a spiritual song."

Finally, before partaking of sleep, it is a sacred duty to give thanks to God, having enjoyed His grace

---

*This sentence begins the disputed passage.

† This is what Suicer pronounces " a most irrelevant question and one worthy only of a Cabalist." No doubt the reader will agree with this criticism.

130

and love, and so go straight to sleep. "And confess to Him in songs of the lips," he says, "because in His command all His good pleasure is done, and there is no deficiency in His salvation." Further among the ancient Greeks, in their banquets over the brimming cups, a song was sung called a skolion, after the manner of the Hebrew psalms, all together raising the pean with the voice, and sometimes also taking turns in the song while they drank healths round; while those that were more musical than the rest sang to the lyre. But let amatory songs be banished far away, and let our songs be hymns to God. "Let them praise," it is said, "His name in the dance, and let them play to Him on the timbrel and psaltery." And what is the choir which plays? The Spirit will show thee: "Let His praise be in the congregation (church) of the saints; let them be joyful in their King." And again He adds, "The Lord will take pleasure in His people." For temperate harmonies are to be admitted; but we are to banish as far as possible from our robust mind those liquid harmonies, which, through pernicious arts in the modulation of tones, train to effeminacy and scurrility. But grave and modest strains say farewell to the turbulence of drunkenness. Chromatic harmonies are therefore to be abandoned to immodest revels, and to florid and meretricious music.

Now, without entering into the merits of Suicer's arguments in proof that the passage is spurious, or those of Bingham in proof that it does not refer to worship, I here submit a collation of facts from that part of the chapter which is unquestionably genuine and which show, beyond all cavil, that Clement either did not intend, by the passage in dispute or by any other statement, to countenance the use of instrumental music in Christian worship, or he positively contradicts himself one or the other. That he did oppose, in strong and unmistakable terms, such use of instrumental music, may be clearly seen from the following facts, which my readers can verify for themselves by looking carefully over the chapter quoted:

1. Such instruments as the pipe and flute are "more suitable to beasts than men," are incompatible with "the temperate banquet," and are, therefore, "to be banished from" such assemblies.

2. He refers to such music as "licentious and mischievous" and advocates its exclusion from temperate feasts on the ground that Christians should "guard against whatever pleasure titillates eye and ear."

3. Although he quotes David's command to praise the Lord with the trumpet, the psaltery, the lyre, the timbrel and dance, chords and organ, and clashing cymbals, yet he immediately follows it with a symbolic explanation of the whole thing by saying that, with Christians, "the tongue is the psaltery of the Lord," "the mouth" is "the lyre," praising on "the timbrel and dance refers to the church meditating on the resurrection of the dead," and the human "body" is the "organ" and its "nerves are the strings."

4. After saying that "man is truly a pacific instru-

ment," he says "other instruments, if you investigate, you will find to be warlike, inflaming to lust," and he then mentions the different kinds of instruments employed by the warlike nations among the ancients.

5. Then, in contrast with this variety of carnal instruments used by different belligerent nations, he not only says that "the word alone" is "the one instrument of peace" by which Christians "honor God," but he specifically declares that they "no longer employ the ancient psaltery, and trumpet, and timbrel, and flute" which "contemners of the fear of God were wont to make use of."

Now, in view of such an array of incontrovertible facts, let us ask, in all sincerity, would any rational and pious mind utter such statements as the foregoing, and then teach, in the same breath, that men may, with propriety, use instrumental music in the worship of God? All right reason refuses to believe it. Moreover, even if it be admitted that the alleged spurious passage was written by Clement, it is still a fact that, while, in it, he is represented as saying "play to Him on the psaltery of ten strings," yet, in the very same connection, he is represented as giving it all a symbolic turn by asking: "Does not the ten-stringed psaltery indicate the word Jesus?" In the language of A. Cleveland Coxe, author of Notes on Clement of Alexandria, who, commenting on the opening sentence of the passage in dispute, says: "Here instrumental music is allowed, though he turns everything into a type.'' But, in view of all his utterances, both figurative and unfigurative, it is simply impossible to interpret Clement in support of instrumental music in Christian worship without involving him in unaccountable self-contradiction. No man, with the intelligence, learning and piety for which the eminent Alexandrian was noted, and at whose feet the learned and renowned Origen once sat as a pupil, would be guilty of such gross inconsistency and absurdity.

We conclude, therefore, and with good reason, that those who resort to Ambrose and Clement for support of the practice in question are leaning on a broken stick.

CHAPTER XIII.

Music Among the Jews—A Parallel Controversy.

It is a well-known fact that the absence of instrumental music from the Jewish worship as that worship obtained in the synagogue of New Testament times, has often been used, and very properly so, as favoring the opposition to the practice among Christians. The force of this argument is derived from the fact, generally understood and admitted, that the worship of the church of Christ was patterned after that of the Jewish synagogue. Chambers' Encyclopedia bears the following testimony:

On the connection between the Jewish synagogue and the Christian church, and their respective rites and modes of worship, we cannot here enlarge. This much, however, we may say, that it is obvious to the most superficial observation that the principal practices of the latter belong, with certain modifications, to the former; and it has been conjectured that even the melodies of certain hymns still sung in the Roman churches are to be traced to the temple and the synagogues. It is, moreover, well known that the early Christian churches were entirely organized after the pattern of the synagogues.—*Vol.* IX., p. 254.

It is no part of my purpose in this chapter to present a general history of music among the Jews, but rather to present the leading facts of an interesting and instructive parallel controversy over the music question that has gone on among the Jews simultaneously with that, on the same subject, among Christians. Few persons, comparatively, are aware of the extent to which this same disturbing question has been a bone of contention among the Jewish people, or of the bitterness, strife and division which it has caused among them. In fact, while the controversy among Christians has been more widespread than among Jews, yet among the latter it has been equally bitter and relentless, leading, in some instances, to open rupture of fellowship and a final appeal to the civil courts to determine the question of property rights. In these respects, the reader will be impressed with the striking parallel between the course of Israel's descendants in regard to this vexed question, and the unfortunate and sometimes disgraceful proceedings which have frequently marked the course of professed Christians over the same matter.

Be it observed, first of all, that instrumental music was no part of the worship in the ancient Jewish synagogue. It was never used in that worship. It is as much of an innovation in the synagogue worship of modern times as it is in the worship of the church of Christ. That it was used in the worship of what is called Judaism proper, that is, in the ancient temple worship, is a fact freely admitted by both Jews and Christians. Moreover, it is a significant fact that, just as Christians charge their fellow-Christians with *judaizing* or *imitating the Jews* when they introduce instrumental music into the worship of the church, so Jews charge their fellow-Jews with *imitating the Christians* when they introduce that practice into the worship of the synagogue. When that learned Roman Catholic theologian and scholastic doctor of the thirteenth century, Thomas Aquinas, quoted elsewhere in this work, said: "Our church does not use musical instruments, as harps and psalteries, to praise God withal, that she may not seem to Judaize"* (*Bingham's Antiq. Vol. 2, p.* 483, *London Ed.*), little did he dream that, in a few centuries, this secularizing innovation would gain such a footing among Christians that those Jews, remaining loyal to their ancient synagogue worship, would have occasion to charge their fellow-Jews, who might adopt it, with *imitating Christians!* But this is precisely the state of things that has come to pass.

That my readers may have before them the facts concerning this interesting charge and counter-charge between Christians and Jews, with also a statement of the controversy among the latter, I here insert some extracts from the Jewish Encyclopedia, a learned and voluminous work brought out in re-

---

*Ecclesia nostra non assumit instrumenta musica, sicut cith-aras et psalteria, in divinas laudes, ne videatur Judaizare.—Quaets. XCI., Art. ii.

cent years under the editorship of Isidore Singer. From these extracts, the reader will see when the disturbing practice in question was first introduced into the synagogue worship, and also the confusion, strife and division which it created. This learned Jewish authority testifies as follows:

1. The modern organ in Reform Synagogues as an accessory of worship was first introduced by Israel Jacobson at Berlin in the new house of prayer which he opened for the Shabu'ot festival, June 14, 1815. It aroused great indignation and opposition on the part of the rest of the community, a successful appeal being made to Emperor Frederic William III. to close the place, on the plea that the Reform schism was detrimental to the established rights of the Jewish Church, and was especially disturbing to the Jewish congregation of Berlin. The house was closed December 6, 1815. The members of the Reform party succeeded in building and dedicating their first temple on October 18, 1818, at Hamburg, where they set up a fine organ, but employed a non-Jewish organist. * * * The objectors based their prohibition of the organ in the synagogue on the following grounds: (1) Playing on musical instruments is prohibited on Sabbaths and holy days, and even to engage a non-Jew to play for Jews on Sabbath is considered a "shebut" or disturbance of the Sabbath rest; (2) music, except at marriage ceremonies, is generally prohibited, in token of mourning for the destruction of Jerusalem; (3) Jewish divine services must not be made to imitate the customs of the Christian Church.—*Jewish Encyclopedia, Vol. IX., p.* 432.

2. Among the Reform congregations in the United States the organ was first introduced in 1840 in Temple Beth Elohim at Charleston, S. C., under Rabbi Gustav Posnanski, by a vote of 46 against 40 of the older members, who objected to the innovation and who in 1844 carried the matter into the courts. The decision was against the minority, who appealed the case; and the higher court affirmed the decision in 1846. In the opinion, written by Judge Butler, the court held that, being unable to decide the merits of this religious controversy, it must rely upon the judgment of the majority of the congregation (text of decision in Ezra's Collection, "The Jews of South Carolina," article VIII., "The Organ in the Synagogue"). The minority finally withdrew and organized a separate congregation.—*Ibid.* pp. 432, 433.

3. Instrumental music is quite a modern feature in synagogal worship. Owing to the rabbinical "fence" which prohibited the use of an instrument on Sabbath and festivals because of the probability that it would require tuning or other preparation, it is still avoided by conservative congregations on those days. Much controversy has raged about this point in Jewish as in other communities. The earlier hesitation of the church to adopt the organ because it was "a Jewish instrument" has been reproduced in the assumption of many Jews that it was specifically a Christian one. It is still banned by rigid adherents to old ways; but in ordinary conservative congregations it is unhesitatingly employed at weddings and other services on week days. —*Ibid.* p. 134.

On the general character of Hebrew music, the American Cyclopedia says:

The Hebrew music, both vocal and instrumental, is constantly referred to in the Bible, and especially in the Psalms, and yet we have no certain knowledge as to its character. It was probably founded on the music of the Egyptians, and it is conjectured that one of the results of the Egyptian training which Moses received was the introduction into the Hebrew service of the music of the Egyptian priesthood. But no melodies that have come down to us can be identified as those used in the temple service. That the singers were a body by themselves under leaders, and that the singing was done by alternate choirs, as was later the case with the primitive Christians, is well known. That they had various instruments, both wind and stringed, is also known. —*Vol. XII. p.* 87, *Art. Music.*

On the same subject, the Schaff-Herzog Encyclopedia deposes as follows:

The cultivation of sacred music, which was commenced under Samuel, especially through the establishment of the school of the prophets (1 Sam. 10: 5; 19: 19, 20), reached its height under David, who, encouraged and assisted by the choir of the prophets (2 Chron. 29: 25), was not only an expert in song and music himself, but also an inventor of musical instruments, as may be seen from Amos 6: 5.—Vol. 2, p. 1598, *Art. Music and Musical Instruments.*

Piety and religious devotion were prominent graces among the ancient Hebrews, a fact well attested by their conduct even as exiles in a foreign land, as exhibited in the following inspired poem:

By the rivers of Babylon,
There we sat down, yea, we wept,
When we remembered Zion.
Upon the willows in the midst thereof
We hanged up our harps.
For there they that led us captive
Required of us songs,
And they that wasted us,
Required of us mirth, saying,
Singing us one of the songs of Zion.
How shall we sing Jehovah's song
In a foreign land?
If I forget thee, O Jerusalem,
Let my right hand forget her skill.
Let my tongue cleave to the
Roof of my mouth,
If I remember thee not;
If I prefer not Jerusalem
Above my chief joy.—*Psa. 137: 1-6.*

It was this beautiful sentiment of devotion to Jehovah, and to the worship of Jehovah, which, after their return from the Babylonish captivity, led to the erection of numerous synagogues throughout Palestine and in all other countries whither the Jews were dispersed. Of these synagogues and the use made of them, George P. Fisher says:

The centers of Jewish instruction and worship were the synagogues, which sprung up during and after the Exile. They were found not only in Palestine, but also in all the towns of the Roman Empire of any considerable size, where Jews resided. The buildings were plain, rectangular edifices, either placed on an eminence or marked by a pole rising from the roof. The synagogues were under the management of "elders." In them, on the Sabbath, all faithful Jews met for prayer, and to hear and to study the law.—*History of the Christian Church,* pp. 15, 16.

As elsewhere observed, the order of organization and worship in the synagogue became the model for organization and worship in the church of Christ. Smith's Dictionary of the Bible says:

It will be enough, in this place, to notice in what way the ritual, no less than the organization, was connected with the facts of the New Testament history, and with the life and order of the Christian Church. Here, too, we meet with multiplied coincidences. It would hardly be an exaggeration to say that the worship of the Church was identical with that of the Synagogue, modified (1) by the new truths, (2) by the new institution of the Supper of the Lord, (3) by the spiritual *Charismata.—Vol. IV., pp.* 3136, 3137.

Thus, we see that, greatly similar in organization and worship, the Synagogue and the Church have had similar fortunes in battling against innovation; and whatever else may be thought of the vivid parallel between the Jewish and Christian communities on the music question, the reader must be deeply impressed with the similarity of effort on the part of conservatives in both cases to preserve inviolate the divine order as it came from inspired men.

CHAPTER XIV.

Testimony of Specialists, Encyclopedists, Historians, and Commentators.

Our general theme has elicited attention from all classes of Biblical writers in all ages, and the mass of literature which has accumulated on the subject, in ancient and modern times, is an irrefutable proof of the importance attached to it in different ages by competent critics. In an effort to present, within reasonable limits, a fair consensus of judgment among those who have spoken, it is not always an easy task to decide what to introduce and what to omit; but it is the aim, in the present chapter, to give representative statements from specialists, encyclopedists, historians, and commentators who, although occupying different fields of research, nevertheless speak with great unanimity when they have occasion to discuss our theme. We shall now hear from them in their own language, and in the following order:

I. SPECIALISTS.

We present, first of all, the testimony of a group of scholars properly termed specialists in the music realm. It may be observed, in passing, that all of those here presented, without exception, as far as we have been able to ascertain, favored the use of instrumental music in the worship, but were compelled, for truth's sake, to speak as they have spoken, and their testimony is, therefore, the more valuable.

1. DR. FREDERIC LOUIS RITTER, Director of the School of Music at Vassar College, in his "History of Music from the Christian Era to the Present Time," says:

We have no real knowledge of the exact character of the music which formed a part of the religious devotion of the first Christian congregations. It was, however, purely vocal. Instrumental music was excluded, at first, as having been used by the Romans at their depraved festivities; and everything reminding them of heathen worship could not be endured by the new religionists. As late as the fourth century, St. Hieronymus says, speaking of the degraded state of Roman spectacles, "A Christian maid should not know what a lyre or flute is, nor what their use is." This strict confinement to purely vocal music was, however, more adhered to in the churches of the Occident; for in the Orient, with the multiplication of Christian congregations, the custom of introducing instrumental music in the church service, after the manner of the heathen, became more and more general.—P. 28.

2. EDWARD DICKINSON, Professor of the History of Music, in the Conservatory of Music, Oberlin College, says:

While the Greek and Roman songs were metrical, the Christian psalms were antiphons, prayers, responses, etc., were unmetrical; and while the pagan melodies were always sung to an instrumental accompaniment, the church chant was exclusively vocal. Through the influence of this double change of technical and æsthetic basis, the liturgic song was at once more free, aspiring, and varied than its prototype, taking on that rhythmic flexibility and delicate shading in which also the unique charm of the Catholic chant of the present day so largely consists.

In view of the controversies over the use of instrumental music in worship, which have been so violent in the British and American Protestant churches, it is an interesting question whether instruments were employed by the primitive Christians. We know that instruments performed an important function in the Hebrew temple service and in the ceremonies of the Greeks. At this point, however, a break was made with all previous practice, and although the lyre and flute were sometimes employed by the Greek converts, as a general rule the use of instruments in worship was condemned. Many of the fathers, speaking of religious song, make no mention of instruments; others, like Clement of Alexandria and St. Chrysostom, refer to them only to denounce them. Clement says: "Only one instrument do we use, *viz.* the word of peace wherewith we honor God, no longer the old psaltery, trumpet, drum, and flute." Chrysostom exclaims: "David formerly sang in psalms, also we sing to-day with him; he had a lyre with lifeless strings, the church has a lyre with living strings. Our tongues are the strings of the lyre, with a different tone, indeed, but with a more accordant piety." St. Ambrose expresses his scorn for those who would play the lyre and psaltery instead of singing hymns and psalms; and St. Augustine adjures believers not to turn their hearts to theatrical instruments. The religious guides of the early Christians felt that there would be an incongruity, and even profanity, in the use of the sensuous nerve-exciting effects of instrumental sound in their mystical, spiritual worship. Their high religious and moral enthusiasm needed no aid from external stimulus; the pure vocal utterance was the more proper expression of their faith. —*Music in the History of the Western Church*, pp. 54, 55.

3. JOHN SPENCER CURWEN, member of the Royal Academy of Music and President (in 1880) of the Tonic Sol-fa College, London, bears the following testimony:

Men still living can remember the time when organs were very seldom found outside the Church of England. The Methodists, Independents, and Baptists rarely had them, and by the Presbyterians they were stoutly opposed. But since these bodies began to introduce organs, the adoption of them has been unchecked. Even the Presbyterians are giving away, and if we read the future by the past, we can hardly doubt that, in a few years, unaccompanied singing will very seldom be heard. Yet, even in the Church of England itself, organs did not obtain admission without much controversy.—*Studies in Worship Music*, p. 179.

From the testimony of this eminent authority, the reader can see that *all* denominations have had the

146

same experience with this innovation. They opposed it at first, but by and by yielded to the popular clamor for it. Moreover, it must be apparent to the thoughtful that one clear statement from the New Testament authorizing the practice, or one example of its use by any church under apostolic leadership, would have forestalled all the controversy, and set the question at rest. The same is true of pouring or sprinkling for baptism. One clear utterance of inspired men, authorizing the practice, or one example of it under their leadership would have forestalled all controversy and set the question at rest. The reason why singing and immersion are not in controversy is because there is divine authority for them; but for instrumental music in worship, and pouring and sprinkling for baptism, there is simply no divine authority; and hence, so long as either is practiced and contended for, so long will there be controversy and division even to the end of time.

On the *overestimated value* of the organ in worship, this same eminent authority, although decidedly in favor of the instrument as thus used, gives the following frank and impartial testimony:

The organ is spoken of as "the king of instruments," "the church orchestra," etc. Its undoubtedly fine qualities are praised to such an extent that its defects are forgotten. It is, however, highly important that we should impartially weigh its strong and weak points. Its most serious defect for the purpose of congregational music is want of accent. It cannot give more stress to one note than to another, and the very name in music for a tone which is equally loud during its whole length is "organ tone." Singing led by an organ always becomes monotonous and heavy and loses its accent. The *crescendo* and *diminuendo* of the swell organ must not for a moment be confused with what is here meant by accent.—*Same Work,* pp. 184, 185.

Finally, on page 186 of the same work, we have the very best that this master of music can say in defense of the organ in worship, as follows:

The real value of the organ, when properly used, is that it floods the building with sound, so that timid worshipers are encouraged to sing. They are encouraged because they do not hear their own voices, and because it is easier to sing when the way is smoothed by instrumental accompaniment. The musical effect, also, is improved by the organ; harsh and loud voices are leveled; the interstices, as it were, are filled up, and the congregational voice is rounded into harmonious unity.

That which "floods the building with sound" and prevents the worshipers from "hearing their own voices," not only cannot help in obeying the command to "teach and admonish one another" in song, but hinders from obeying it.

4. ADOLPH BERNARD MARX, at one time Professor of Music in the University of Berlin, and the author of several works on vocal and instrumental music, speaking of the character of organ music, says:

The want of elasticity in organ tone is most noticeable in this, that consecutive sounds are not only not merged and blended as is the case with stringed and wind instruments and the singing voice, but that they admit no *crescendo* or *decrescendo,* no change from *forte* to *piano,* except through what can be obtained from various registering of the whole. Every sound of the organ, the softest as well as the strongest, is hard and unchangeable like a column, and is, in spite of its natural strength and sweetness, lifeless. While, on the other hand, all living things are forever changing, transforming, waxing and waning, consolidating, inflecting, and even testify to their vitality by sinking and rising again, thus claiming our immediate sympathy as the echoes of the pulsation of our own mind. In this respect, therefore, the organ is unsympathetic and foreign to our innermost life, of which, as of all other life, the chief characteristic is motion and change. In every voice, in every combination of voices, the organ gives us the same unchanged expression, and every individual sound from first to last is unvarying and rigid, however soft and sweet its material may be. This is the unsympathetic and nonhuman, because unliving, aspect of this instrument, so admired in other respects.—*Quoted in Studies in Worship Music, p.* 185.

5. SAMUEL WILLOUGHBY DUFFIELD, author of "Latin Hymn Writers and Their Hymns," himself an ardent advocate of instrumental music in worship, says:

Another question now meets us, and one of some importance: Did the early Christians employ any musical instrument? In reply, it can be noted that ψάλλειν, "to make melody," is usually taken to refer to a musical accompaniment. In Rom. 15: 9 it is a quotation from Psa. 18: 50, where it means, "I will *sing psalms.*" In 1 Cor. 14: 15 ("I will *sing* with the spirit, and I will *sing* with the understanding also") and in Jas. 5: 13 ("Is any merry? let him *sing psalms*") we have nothing decisive except that we know that the Jewish method of "singing psalms" was to the accompaniment of musical instruments. Thus, with all these texts before us, we are not able either to affirm or deny the fact. The reference of Paul (1 Cor. 14: 7) to the *pipe* (αὐλός, flute) and harp (κιθάρα, lute) gives us no assistance. The "harp" of Revelation 5: 8; 14: 2, and 15: 2, is the cithara or lute again, but neither does this tell us what the early Christians did or did not do. The inference is pretty strong that they avoided some things that were Jewish—and instrumental music was a marked feature in the Jews' worship—but it is plain that (as with the Sabbath question) there was a great deal of blending at the edges between the two dispensations. —*Latin Hymn Writers and Their Hymns,* p. 67.

6. FRANK LANDON HUMPHREYS, author of "The Evolution of Church Music," gives this testimony:

One of the features which distinguishes the Christian religion from almost all others is its quietness; it aims to repress the outward signs of inward feeling. Savage instinct, and the religion of Greece also, had employed the rhythmic dance and all kinds of gesticulatory motions to express the inner feelings, some of them entirely unsuitable to purposes of worship. The early Christians discouraged all outward signs of excitement, and from the very beginning, in

150

the music they used, reproduced the spirit of their religion—an inward quietude. All the music employed in their early services was vocal, and the rhythmic element and all gesticulation were forbidden.—*Evolution of Church Music*, p. 42.

7. SIR JOHN HAWKINS. This noted specialist in the department of the history of music, another strong advocate of instrumental music in the worship, testifies as follows:

With respect to the music of the primitive church, though it consisted in the singing of psalms and hymns, yet was it performed in sundry different manners; that is to say, sometimes the psalms were sung by one person alone, the rest hearing with attention; sometimes they were sung by the whole assembly; sometimes alternately, the congregation being for that purpose divided into separate choirs; and, lastly, by one person, who repeated the first part of the verse, the rest joining in the close thereof.— *History of Music*, Vol. I. p. 108.

According to this authority, though "the singing" was "performed in sundry different manners," yet it was all *singing*, and *no instrumental music*.

II. ENCYCLOPEDISTS.

Under this head, we present the testimony of scholars whose business it is to make an impartial record of facts concerning the great variety and multiplicity of subjects embraced within their scope. Considering their ability and eminence, what they say is certainly significant; and we will now hear from them in the following order:

1. The American Cyclopedia:

Pope Vitalian is related to have first introduced organs into some of the churches of western Europe, about 670; but the earliest trustworthy account is that of the 'one sent as a present by the Greek emperor Constantine Copronymus to Pepin, king of the Franks, in 755.—*Vol. 12, p. 688.*

2. Schaff-Herzog Encyclopedia:

In the Greek Church the organ never came into use. But after the eighth century it became more and more common in the Latin Church; not, however, without opposition from the side of the monks. Its misuse, however, raised so great an opposition to it, that, but for the Emperor Ferdinand, it would probably have been abolished by the Council of Trent. The Reformed Church discarded it; and though the Church of Basel very early reintroduced it, it was in other places admitted only sparingly, and after long hesitation.—*Vol. 2, p. 1702.*

3. The New International Encyclopedia:

The organ is said to have been first employed in the church during the time of Pope Vitalian I. (c. 666 A.D.). Pepin placed the Constantine organ in the church of St. Corneille at Compiègne, and Charlemagne had one made at Aix-la-Chapelle, a model of the one at Compiègne.—Vol. XIII., p. 446.

ENCYCLOPEDISTS, HISTORIANS, AND COMMENTATORS.

4. McClintock and Strong's Cyclopedia:

The Greek word ψάλλω is applied among the Greeks of modern times exclusively to sacred music, which in the Eastern Church has never been any other than vocal, instrumental music being unknown in that Church, as it was in the primitive Church. Sir John Hawkins, following the Romish writers in his erudite work on the *History of Music,* makes pope Vitalian, in A.D. 660, the first who introduced organs into churches. But students of ecclesiastical archæology are generally agreed that instrumental music was not used in churches till a much later date; for Thomas Aquinas, A.D. 1250, has these remarkable words: "Our Church does not use musical instruments, as harps and psalteries, to praise God withal, that she may not seem to Judaize." From this passage we are surely warranted in concluding that there was no ecclesiastical use of organs in the time of Aquinas. It is alleged that Marinus Sanutus, who lived about A.D. 1290, was the first that brought the use of wind organs into churches, and hence he received the name of *Torcellus.* In the East, the organ was in use in the emperor's courts, probably from the time of Julian, but never has either the organ or any other instrument been employed in public worship in Eastern churches; nor is mention of instrumental music found in all their liturgies, ancient or modern.—Vol. VIII., p. 739.

5. Chambers' Encyclopedia:

The organ is said to have been first introduced into church music by Pope Vitalian I. in 666. In 757, a great organ was sent as a present to Pepin by the

Byzantine emperor, Constantine Copronymus, and placed in the church of St. Corneille at Compiègne. —Vol. VII., p. 112.

6. A CONCISE CYCLOPEDIA OF RELIGIOUS KNOWL-EDGE:

Instrumental accompaniments date back from the days of St. Ambrose, and some also accredit him with the introduction of antiphonal singing, while others give it to St. Hilary, of Poitiers, who borrowed it from the practice of the Eastern Church.—Page 649.

Then, under the article "organ," on page 683, the same work further says:

The organ has never been used among the Greeks. From the time of Charlemagne organs seem to have come more and more into use in the West, though protests were made against them, and the monks were very averse to their use. At the Reformation they were discarded, being considered "the vilest remnants of Popery;" but they were reintroduced at the Council of Basel.

7. JOHNSON'S UNIVERSAL CYCLOPEDIA:

The organ is said to have been introduced into the church by Pope Vitalian in the seventh century, but its employment in church services probably dates from a much earlier period. Organs were certainly used in churches very commonly in the time of the Carlovingians. We read of organs being sent to King Pepin and Charlemagne as presents by the Byzantine emperors.—*Vol. VI., p.* 335.

8. ENCYCLOPEDIA BRITANNICA:

Though the church from time to time appropriated the secular art forms from their rise to their maturity, its chief authorities were always jealous of these advances, and issued edicts against them. So in 1322 Pope John XXII. denounced the encroachments of counterpoint, alleging that the voluptuous harmony of 3ds and 6ths was fit but for profane uses.—Vol. 17, p. 84, *Art. Music.*

9. FESSENDEN'S ENCYCLOPEDIA:

1. *Vocal music.* This species, which is the most natural, may be considered to have existed before any other. It was continued by the Jews and it is the only kind that is permitted in the Greek and Scotch churches or with few exceptions, in dissenting congregations in England. The Christian rule requires its use both for personal and social edification, Eph. V., Col. iii. The vocal music of the imperial choristers in St. Petersburg incomparably surpasses in sweetness and effect the sounds produced by the combined power of the most exquisite musical instruments. 2. *Instrumental music* is also of very ancient date, its invention being ascribed to Tubal, the sixth descendant from Cain. That instrumental music was not practiced by the primitive Christians, but was an aid to devotion of later times, is evident from church history.—P. 852, *Art. Music.*

10. LONDON ENCYCLOPEDIA:

Pope Vitalianus in 658 introduced the organ into the Roman Churches to accompany the singers. Leo II. in 682 reformed the singing of the psalms and hymns, accommodating the intonation of them to the manner in which they are sung or performed at the present day.—*Vol.* 15, *p.* 280, *Art. Music.*

11. BIBLICAL ENCYCLOPEDIA, on Eph. 5: 19 and Col. 3: 16:

Psalms, either the psalms of the Old Testament, or a sacred song similar to them in character. *Hymns,* Christian songs of praise. And *songs,* perhaps songs of a more personal character, like Simeon's *Nunc dimittis,* or Paul's swan song (2 Tim. 4: 6-8). *Singing* and making melody with your heart to the Lord, the heart moving devoutly with the voice. * * * The design of public worship may be learned from the word worship itself. 1. There is in the constitution of our nature a necessity for the expression of emotion. 2. Audible worship is enjoined. 3. We have divine example—Jesus prayed audibly—and sang with His disciples at the last Supper. 4. There is apostolic example. 5. We have the example of the early church, and of the universal church to this day. 6. Without audible prayer and praise there can be no social worship. * * * Teaching and admonishing one another. The spiritual importance of Christian hymnody comes out impressively here. It is no mere luxury of devotion, certainly no mere musical pleasure; it is an ordained vehicle of instruction and warning. * * * On one of the days when President Garfield lay dying at the seaside, he was a little better, and was permitted to sit by the window, while Mrs. Garfield was in the adjoining room. Love, hope, and gratitude filled her heart as she sang the hymn commencing, "Guide me, O Thou great Jehovah!" As the soft and plaintive notes floated into the sick chamber, the President turned his eyes up to Dr. Bliss, and asked, "Is that Crete?" "Yes," replied the Doctor; "it is Mrs. Garfield." "Quick, open the door a little," anxiously responded the sick man. Dr. Bliss opened the door, and after listening a few moments Mr. Garfield exclaimed, as the large tears coursed down his sunken cheeks, "Glorious, Bliss, isn't it?"—Vol. V. pp. 283, 332.

12. THE CATHOLIC ENCYCLOPEDIA:

To praise God in public worship through songs or hymns in the widest meaning of the word (see hymns) is a custom which the primitive Christians brought with them from the synagogue. For that reason the ecclesiastical songs of the Christians and the Jews in the first centuries after Christ are essentially similar. They consisted mainly of the psalms and the canticles of the Old and New Testaments.—Vol. VII., p. 597.

It is a remarkable fact, particularly noted, as we have seen, by a number of the foregoing encyclopedias, that the Greek Church, which has continued to speak the Greek language to the present day, has always rejected pouring and sprinkling for baptism, and the use of instrumental music in the worship; and they do this, being perfectly familiar with the words *baptizo* (βαπτίζω) and *psallo* (ψάλλω) as used both in the New Testament and in Modern Greek in which these words are still current. This fact is certainly a significant comment on the meaning of these words. Modern Greek is the language still spoken by native Greeks, many of whom have come, in recent years, to the United States, especially to the larger cities. A number of them have located in Louisville, Ky., and they still use these words as meaning, respectively, to *dip* and to *sing*.*

III. Historians.

We next introduce that large and interesting class of witnesses—ecclesiastical or church Historians, whose province it is to furnish a faithful record of facts connected with religious affairs as they have transpired since the establishment of the church.

1. Eusebius. This author, who lived during the latter part of the third and first part of the fourth century, is styled, by way of preëminence, the father of ecclesiastical historians. He makes a number of references to the simplicity which characterized the lives and worship of the early Christians. Referring to the famous letter of Pliny the Second to the emperor Trajan informing him about the Christians, he says:

At the same time he informed him that as far as he had ascertained, they did nothing wicked or con-

---

*In conversation with a company of them, who could speak broken English, the author wrote two brief sentences, one containing *baptizo* (Βαπτίζω) and the other *psallo* (ψάλλω), asking for the meaning of these words. Concerning the former, they promptly replied in terms which, with a certain motion of the hands, meant to put under the water; and concerning the latter, they proceeded to indicate its meaning by humming or chanting a tune.

trary to the laws; except that they rose with the morning sun, and sang a hymn to Christ as to a God. —*Eccles. Hist., Book* III., *Chap.* 33.

2. NEANDER:

Church psalmody, also, passed over from the synagogue into the Christian Church. The Apostle Paul exhorts the primitive churches to sing spiritual songs. For this purpose were used the psalms of the Old Testament, and partly *hymns composed expressly for this object,* especially hymns of praise and of thanks to God and to Christ, such having been known to Pliny, as in customary use among the Christians of his time.—*General Church History,* Vol. I., p. 414.

3. MOSHEIM:

The Christian worship consisted in hymns, prayers, the reading of the Scriptures, a discourse addressed to the people, and concluded with the celebration of the Lord's Supper.—*Eccl. Hist.,* Vol. I., p. 303

Referring to the changes that took place even before the close of the fourth century, the same authority says:

The public prayers had now lost much of that solemn and majestic simplicity, that characterized them in the primitive times, and which were, at present, degenerating into a vain and swelling bombast.—*Vol. I., p.* 304.

4. HENRY HART MILMAN:

Like the rest of the service, the music of the church no doubt grew up from a rude and simple, to a more splendid and artificial form. The practice of singing hymns is coeval with Christianity; the hearers of the apostles sang the praises of God; and the first sound which reached the Pagan ear from the secluded sanctuaries of Christianity was the hymn to Christ as God. * * * The first change in the manner of singing was the substitution of singers, who became a separate order in the church, for the mingled voices of all ranks, ages, and sexes, which was compared by the great reformer of church music to the glad sound of many waters.—*Hist. of Christianity, Vol. iii., pp.* 406, 409.

5. J. E. RIDDLE:

In the first ages of the Christian Church the psalms were always chanted or sung. In the *Apostolical Constitutions* (Book ii 57), we find it laid down as a rule that one of the officiating ministers should chant or sing (ψαλλέτω) the psalms (ὕμνους) of David, and that the people should join by repeating the ends of the verses. And this regulation is repeated and explained by other writers.—*Christian Antiquities,* p. 384.

In the same work, writing on "organs," the same author says:

These instruments of music were introduced into the Christian church about the ninth century. They were unknown alike to the early church, and to all the ancients. * * * The large wind organ was known, however, long before it was introduced into the churches of the west. It appears, from the testimony of Augustine and others, that it was known in Africa and Spain, as early as the fifth and sixth centuries. The first organ used in a church was one which was received by Charlemagne as a present from the emperor Constantine Michael. * * * In the east, organs were never approved as instruments of sacred music, nor did the use of them continue without opposition in the west.—*Ibid. pp.* 734-736.

6. Johann Joseph Ignatius Döllinger, who, during his life, held the chairs of Theology and Church History, respectively, in the Royal University of Munich and the University of Bonn, and who is said to have been the greatest Catholic writer of the nineteenth century, says:

The mass of the catechumens began with the singing of psalms: in the Latin Church, and in the liturgy of the Constitutions, it commenced with the lecture from the sacred Scriptures, between the parts of which, verses of the psalms were sung, which were thence called responsaries. Pope Celestine I. first introduced into the west, probably after the example of St. Ambrose, the custom of reciting a psalm at the beginning of the mass. In the first ages the psalms were sung by the whole assembly standing; after the fourth century the practice introduced by St. Ambrose from the east was adopted in the west, by which the psalms were sung in alternate chant by the congregation, divided into two choirs. The melodies in which they were sung were simple, almost recitative; but at the end of the fourth century, a more artificial song was introduced into some churches as in that of Milan.—*History of the Church,* Vol. II., pp. 307, 308.

7. HEINRICH ERNST FERDINAND GUERICKE, once Professor in the University of Halle and author of "A Manual of Church History" and "Antiquities of the Church," says:

The example of Christ and His Apostles (Matt. 26: 30, and Acts 16: 25), and also their precepts (Jas. 5: 13; Eph. 5: 19; Col. 3: 16), justify us in considering the custom of singing hymns to be very ancient indeed in the Christian Church. The practice of singing such spiritual songs is said to have been fostered and promoted by so early an authority as Ignatius of Antioch; and it was practiced not only for private edification, but also for the purposes of public worship (*Plinii. Epist. ad Traj. X. 96*), who mentions not only the practice, but also the subject-matter of the hymns.—*Antiq. of the Church,* pp. 202, 203.

8. LYMAN COLEMAN, an eminent Presbyterian author and noted for vast learning and accurate scholarship, says:

The organ constituted no part of the furniture of the ancient churches. The first instance on record of its use in the church, occurred in the time of Charlemagne, who received one as a present from Constantine Michael, which was set up in the church at Aix-la-Chapelle. The musicians of this city, and of Mentz, learned to play on the organ in Italy, from which it appears that they were already known in that country.—*Antiquities of the Christian Church,* p. 192.

9. ALZOG, the eminent Catholic Scholar and Church Historian of the University of Freiburg, though fa-

voring the use of instrumental music in worship, nevertheless bears testimony which shows its corruption of the original practice. He says:

St. *Ambrose* and St. *Gregory* rendered great service to church music by the introduction of what are known as the *Ambrosian* and *Gregorian* chants. The latter, composed of notes of equal duration (*cantus firmus, Romanus*), is, in many respects, very similar to our present *choral* chant. The Ambrosian chant, with notes of unequal duration, has more the character of a *recitative*. The Gregorian chant, so dignified and solemn, was taught and brought to perfection in a *school* founded by the excellent Pope from whom it derives its name, whence it gradually spread through the whole church. Ecclesiastical chant, departing in some instances from the simple majesty of its original character, became *more artistic,* and, on this account, less heavenly and more profane; and the Fathers of the Church were not slow to censure this corruption of the old and honored church song. Finally, the *organ,* which seemed an earthly echo of the angelic choirs in heaven, added its full, rich, and inspiring notes to the beautiful simplicity of the Gregorian chant.—*Universal Church History,* Vol. I., pp. 696, 697.

10. GEORGE PARK FISHER, Professor of Ecclesiastical History in Yale University, in his "History of the Christian Church," says:

Church music, which at the outset consisted mainly of the singing of the psalms, flourished especially in Syria and at Alexandria. The music was very simple in its character. There was some sort of alternate singing in the worship of Christians, as it is described by Pliny. The introduction of antiphonal singing at Antioch is ascribed by tradition to Ignatius. * * * The primitive Church music was choral and congregational. Hilary, and in the early part of the period, Gregory the Great, were influential in improving church music. The Arians and other heretics embodied their doctrines in verses to be sung. It was to counteract this influence that Chrysostom caused antiphonies and doxologies to be sung in processions. In the West, Ambrose, in his contest with the Arians, taught his congregation to sing antiphonal hymns. The most famous composers were Ephraëm Syrus, Hilary of Poictiers, and Ambrose. There was some opposition to the use of such hymns, on the ground that they were not taken from the Scriptures; and this could only be overcome by age and usage.—pp. 65, 121.

11. THOMAS STACKHOUSE, eminent historian of the Church of England and author of a "New History of the Holy Bible," gives in this work the following testimony:

In all the books of the Old Testament, there is not the least hint given us of any musical instruments employed in funerals. We read indeed of a good deal of mourning for the dead, of mourners hired on purpose, and of the dismal ditties which these people sung, to excite sorrow in others: but the use of music was reckoned an incongruous thing, and nowise comporting with the solemnity of this sad season. Among heathen authors there is frequent mention made of it, as a thing long in use both with the Greeks and Romans; and therefore we may presume, that from these nations it was that the Jews borrowed, and adopted it into their funeral ceremonies. —*Vol.* 5, pp. 426, 427.

12. DR. KARL AUGUST HASE, Professor of Theology at the University of Jena and a voluminous author, though in favor of the instrument in worship, testifies to the constant opposition to all instrumental music of every kind as follows:

The outward forms of religion became gradually more and more imposing. From the ancient temples the incense and many ancient customs of heathenism were transferred to the churches. By the use of tapers and perpetual lamps, the solemnity of nocturnal festivals was combined with the light of day. * * * Soon after, in face of continual opposition to all instrumental music, the organ (ὄργανον), worthy of being the invention of a saint who had listened to the minstrelsy of angels, was brought to Italy from Greece.—*History of the Christian Church*, p. 153.

13. JOHANN KARL LUDWIG GIESELER, eminent as a Professor at the Universities of Bonn and Göttingen and celebrated as a church historian, describing the simplicity of the service in the primitive church, says:

They assembled for worship in private houses; in cities the churches were often divided into several societies each having its particular place of meeting. In the assemblies the exercises consisted in reading the Scriptures of the Old Testament, explanation of what had been read, exhortation, singing, and prayer

(Col. 3: 16; 1 Tim. 4: 13). The letters of Paul, too, were read and sent from one church to another (Col. 4: 16; 1 Thess. 5: 27). The communion was with them an actual evening meal (ἀγάπη) vid. 1 Cor. 11: 20.—*Ecclesiastical History, Vol.* I. pp. 58, 59.

14. CHARLES JOHN VAUGHAN, of the Church of England, member of the New Testament Revision Committee and the author of a work entitled "The Church of the First Days," describing the simple and impressive service of song among the primitive Christians in times of persecution, says:

The well-known words, *And at midnight Paul and Silas* in their dungeon *prayed and sang praises unto God,* have a sweet music in them for anxious and troubled souls. The thought of those *songs in the night;* verses, perhaps, from our own sacred Book of Psalms, so full of appropriate words for the prisoner and the captive; of those prayers in the jail at Philippi, which have been the example and model of so many Christian confessors and martyrs in all times in their long hours of patient suffering for the truth's sake; may well both encourage and shame us; encourage us by its testimony to the living grace of Christ, and yet shame us by the comparison of our luxurious softness with their noble endurance and their bold confession. *The prisoners heard them.* The original language says, *were listening to them.* Strange unwonted sounds must those have been, those prayers and hymns, in a heathen prison: well might they listen!—*Vol. II., pp.* 308, 309.

15. JOHN FLETCHER HURST, in his "History of the Christian Church," says:

The singing was simple, and modeled after the Jewish psalmody. The lower clergy were almost universally the precentors, for the singing of the congregation was regarded as such an integral part of the divine service that only clerical officers should direct it. The music was at no time, and in no place, regarded as the prerogative of the singers. That only was held to be sacred music which the congregation could participate in, either responsively or continuously. The two churches most noted for sacred music in the early period were Antioch in Syria, and the Italian Church of Milan, where Ambrose created the later psalmody of the Western Church. The music of the church was at first simple, but to the old melodies were now added new words, which in many instances found their way into the public services, and had a tendency to displace the older psalmody. * * * The churches soon adopted an elaborate ceremonial. The hymns of Ephraim the Syrian, of Hilary of Pictavium, and of Sedulius, showed traces of the artificiality which now disturbed every factor in the service of the church. The bombastic rhetoric which had ruled in the Roman world since the death of Cicero was now introduced into the Christian pulpit, and the congregation burst forth in applause extravagant enough for a welcome to a chief returning from the conquest of a new province. The assertion of the secular spirit was prompt and thorough.—*Vol. I.,* p. 357.

16. John Kurtz, a German Lutheran scholar and a great church historian, says:

At first church music was simple, artless, recitative. But the rivalry of heretics forced the orthodox church to pay greater attention to the requirements of art. Chrysostom had to declaim against the secularization of church music. More lasting was the opposition of the church to the introduction of instrumental accompaniment.—*Church History,* Vol. I., p. 376.

The same author, commenting on the great revolution in church music that had taken place by the opening of the nineteenth century, says:

Church music, too, now reached its lowest ebb. The old chorales were altered into modern forms. A multitude of new, unpopular melodies, difficult of comprehension, with a bold school tone were introduced; the last trace of the old rhythm disappeared, and a weary monotony began to prevail, in which all force and freshness were lost. As a substitute, secular preludes, interludes, and concluding pieces were brought in. The people often entered the churches during the playing of operatic overtures, and were dismissed amid the noise of a march or waltz.—Vol. III., p. 153.

17. Edmond de Pressense, pronounced by competent judges an able scholar and a brilliant historian, says:

The church does not remain satisfied, as at first, with singing the psalms. Christian feeling finds expression in its own spiritual song. This utterance, like prayer and the word of edification, proceeds in the first instance from individual inspiration. "If any man hath a psalm," says the apostle, "let him speak," Eph. 5: 19; Col. 3: 16; 1 Cor. 14: 26. Here the reference is evidently to a new song given by inspiration of the Spirit of God to one in the assembly.—*The Early Years of Christianity*, p. 372.

18. PHILIP SCHAFF, the distinguished President of the American Company of New Testament Revisers, and one of the greatest scholars of the nineteenth century, in his "History of the Christian Church," says:

The use of organs in churches is ascribed to Pope Vitalian (657-672). Constantine Copronymos sent an organ with other presents to King Pepin of France in 767. Charlemagne received one as a present from the Caliph Haroun al Rashid, and had it put up in the cathedral of Aix-la-Chapelle.   *   *   *
The attitude of the churches toward the organ varies. It shared to some extent the fate of images except that it never was an object of worship.   *   *   *
The Greek Church disapproves the use of organs. The Latin Church introduced it pretty generally, but not without the protest of eminent men, so that even in the Council of Trent a motion was made, though not carried, to prohibit the organ at least in the mass. —*Vol.* IV., p. 439.

19. JOSEPH BINGHAM, the well-known author of *"Antiquities of the Christian Church,"* and said to be one of the greatest scholars the Church of England has ever produced, says:

Music in churches is as ancient as the apostles, but instrumental music not so.

Then, after noting the use of organs in the churches of the thirteenth century, he says:

The use of the instrument, indeed, is much ancienter, but not in church service. * * * In the Western parts, the instrument was not so much as known till the eighth century; for the first organ that was ever seen in France was one sent as a present to King Pepin by Constantinus Copronymus, the Greek emperor (an. 766). * * * But, now, it was only used in princes' courts, and not yet brought into churches; nor was it ever received into the Greek churches, there being no mention of an organ in all their Liturgies, ancient or modern.—*Works, Vol. 2, pp. 482-484, London Ed.*

20. James Craigie Robertson, Professor of Church History in King's College, London, testifies concerning early church music as a means of instruction, as follows:

Psalmody formed a large portion of the early Christian worship. It consisted partly of the Old Testament psalms, and partly of hymns composed on Christian themes; and both in the church and among heretical sects it was found a very effective means of impressing doctrines on the minds of the less educated members.—*History of the Christian Church, Vol. I.,* p. 166.

21. William Jones, the Church Historian, noting the fact that the primitive Christians received from the apostles all the acts of worship, says:

They received from the apostles the various ordinances of public worship, the apostles' doctrine, the fellowship, the breaking of bread, and the ordinances of prayer and praise; and in these they continued steadfastly.—*History of the Christian Church to the Eighteenth Century*, p. 49.

22. GEORGE H. DRYER:

The order of worship seems to have been prayer, reading the Scriptures, prayer, teaching, prophecy, speaking with tongues, singing. Teaching was probably an exposition of the passage read with practical applications, the result of reflection and the attainment of knowledge or gnosis. * * * In time, teaching and prophecy came together and formed the sermon and exhortation. Speaking with tongues passed into the songs and hymns of the Church.— *History of the Christian Church,* Vol. I., p. 243.

23. PHILIP SMITH:

A large part of the service consisted in singing the psalms of the Old Testament, the few but cherished canticles of the New, and the hymns, which were composed not only as the utterance of praise, but as the means of impressing doctrine in a more vivid form on the minds of the worshipers.—*History of the Christian Church During the First Ten Centuries,* Vol. I., p. 195.

24. GEORGE WADDINGTON. Commenting on the letter of Pliny the Younger to the emperor Trajan, this historian of the Church of England, says:

This being justly considerd as the most important document remaining to us in early Christian history, we shall here transcribe some portion of it, the more willingly as we shall have occasion hereafter to refer to it. After mentioning the difficulty of his own situation, and his perplexity in what manner to proceed against men charged with no other crime than the name of Christian, the writer proceeds as follows: "Others were named by an informer, who at first confessed themselves Christians, and afterwards denied it. * * * They affirmed that the whole of their fault or error lay in this—that they were wont to meet together on a stated day before it was light, and sing among themselves alternately a hymn to Christ, as to God, and bind themselves by an oath, not to the commission of any wickedness, but not to be guilty of theft, or robbery, or adultery, never to falsify their word, nor to deny a pledge committed to them when called upon to return it," etc.

After quoting still further from Pliny's letter, Waddington adds his own testimony to its great value as a historic document, as follows:

So few and uncertain are the records left to guide our inquiries through the obscure period which immediately followed the conclusion of the labors of the Apostles, that the above testimony to the numbers and virtues of our forefathers in faith becomes indeed valuable. No history of our Church can be perfect without it; and its clear and unsuspected voice will be listened to by every candid inquirer in every age of truth and history.—*Waddington's History of the Church*, p. 10.

25. William Hetherington:

In the beginning of the year 1562, a meeting of the Convocation was held, in which the subject of further

reformation was vigorously discussed on both sides.
* * * When it was proposed that there should be
some alterations in the Prayer book, a very warm
debate ensued. Six alterations were proposed, * * *
[one of which was] that the use of organs be laid
aside. * * * When the vote came to be taken on
these propositions, forty-three voted for them, and
thirty-five against; but when the proxies were
counted, the balance was turned; the final state of
the vote being fifty-eight for, and fifty-nine against.
Thus it was determined, by the majority of a single
vote, and that the proxy of an absent person who
did not hear the reasoning, that the Prayer book
should remain unimproved, that there should be no
further reformation, that there should be no relief
granted to those whose consciences felt aggrieved by
the admixture of human inventions in the worship
of God.—*History Westminster Assembly of Divines*,
p. 30.

26. Socrates, surnamed "Scholasticus," was the
Greek Church historian who has the distinction of
continuing the subject of ecclesiastical history from
the point where Eusebius closed his history—that is,
from early in the fourth century to near the middle
of the fifth century. So great is the influence that
mere singing has in impressing doctrine and forming
sentiment and character that, as we learn from Socrates and some others, the different religious sects,
which arose during the course of centuries, invariably resorted to it as a means of spreading their principles. He says:

The Arians, as we have said, held their meetings without the city. As often therefore as the festal days occurred, that is to say, the Sabbath and Lord's day* of each week, on which assemblies are usually held in the churches, they congregated within the city gates about the public piazzas, and sang responsive verses adapted to the Arian heresy. This they did during the greater part of the night; and again in the morning, chanting the same responsive compositions, they paraded through the midst of the city, and so passed out of the gates to go to their places of assembly.—*Ecclesiastical History,* Book VI., Chap. VIII., p. 314.

27. Sozomen, another Greek writer of ecclesiastical history and a cotemporary of Socrates, wrote a history of the Church covering the period between the years 323 and 439. Writing on the power of song and the use made of it, he says:

About this time, Apollinarius openly devised a heresy, to which his name has since been given. He induced many persons to secede from the church, and formed separate assemblies. Vitalius, a Presbyter of Antioch, concurred with him in the promulgation of his peculiar opinions. In other respects, Vitalius was blameless in life and conduct, and was zealous in watching over those committed to his pastoral superintendence; hence he was greatly revered by the people. He seceded from communion with Meletius and joined Apollinarius, and presided over those at Antioch who had embraced the same opinions; by the sanctity of his life he attracted a great number

---

* τό τε σάββατον καὶ ἡ κυριακή.

of followers, who are still called Vitalians by the citizens of Antioch. * * * They sang the psalms composed by Apollinarius; for, besides his great attainments in other branches of literature, he was a poet, and by the beauty of his verses he induced many to adopt his sentiments. He composed verses to be sung by men at convivial meetings and at their daily labor, and by women while engaged at the loom. But, whether his songs were adapted for holidays, festivals, or other occasions, they were all alike to the praise and glory of God.—*Ecclesiastical History,* Book VI., Chap. XXV., p. 280.

28. JAMES PIERCE. Although this learned Presbyterian scholar of the eighteenth century, and some others to be presented in this connection, were not Church Historians in the strict sense, yet some of their works are practically of this nature, and it is not improper to hear from them under this head. Writing in the interest of the "Dissenters," this eminent Non-Conformist says:

I come now to say somewhat of the antiquity of musical instruments. But that these were not used in the Christian Church in the primitive times is attested by all the ancient writers with one consent. Hence, they figuratively explain all the places of the Old Testament which speak of musical instruments, as I might easily show by a thousand testimonies out of Clement of Alexandria, Basil, Ambrose, Jerome, Augustine, Chrysostom, and many others. * * * From what has been said, it appears no musical instruments were used in the pure times of the church.—*A Vindication of the Dissenters,* cited by Girardeau, pp. 157, 158.

29. THOMAS AQUINAS, sometimes called the Angelic Doctor, one of the most learned Roman Catholic scholars of the thirteenth century, and a voluminous writer, says:

Our Church does not use musical instruments, as harps and psalteries, to praise God withal, that she may not seem to Judaize.*—*Bingham's Antiquities,* Vol. II., p. 483, *London Edition.*

30. CAJETAN, a Roman Catholic Cardinal and theologian of the sixteenth century, says:

It is to be observed the church did not use organs in Thomas' time; whence, even to this day, the Church of Rome does not use them in the Pope's presence. And truly it will appear that musical instruments are not to be suffered in the ecclesiastical offices we meet together to perform for the sake of receiving internal instruction from God; and so much the rather are they to be excluded, because God's internal discipline exceeds all human disciplines, which rejected this kind of instruments.—*Cited by Girardeau,* pp. 161, 162.

31. JOHANN JAHN. This eminent Oriental scholar and Biblical archæologist of the eighteenth century, after mentioning singing, reading the Scriptures, exhortation, prayer, and a contribution for the poor, as the items of worship in the ancient Jewish synagogue, then states that the items of Christian wor-

---

*Aquin. Secunda Secundae, Quaest. xci. art. ii. *Ecclesia nostra non assumit instrumenta musica, sicut citharas et psalteria, in divinas laudes, ne videatur Judaizare.*

ship, as established by Christ and the apostles, were the same, with the exception that the Lord's Supper was added. His words are:

§399. MODE OF WORSHIP PRACTICED BY THE APOSTLES. It was by ministering in synagogues, that the apostles gathered the first Christians. They retained also essentially the *same mode* of worship with that of the Synagogues, excepting that the Lord's Supper was made an additional institution, agreeably to the example of Christ, Acts 2: 42; 20: 7-11; 1 Cor. 11: 17-34.—*Jahn's Biblical Archæology*, pp. 503, 504.

32. PROFESSOR JOHN GIRARDEAU. In his work on "Music in the Church," written while he was "Professor in Columbia Theological Seminary, South Carolina," this Presbyterian scholar says:

It has thus been proved, by an appeal to historical facts, that the church, although lapsing more and more into defection from the truth and into a corruption of apostolic practice, had no instrumental music for twelve hundred years;* and that the Calvinistic Reformed Church ejected it from its services as an element of Popery, even the Church of England having come very nigh to its extrusion from her worship. The historical argument, therefore, combines with the Scriptural and the confessional to raise a solemn and powerful protest against its employment

---

*He means it did not become general during this period. It was introduced by a few churches at an earlier date, but, precisely as in the case of pouring and sprinkling for baptism, it never became general till nearly a thousand years after its introduction.

by the Presbyterian Church. It is heresy in the sphere of worship.—*Instrumental Music in Public Worship,* p. 179.

IV. COMMENTATORS.

For reasons already mentioned in this work, commentators, as well as some other scholars, sometimes fail to discriminate between the ancient meaning of *psallo,* "to strike the chords of an instrument," and its subsequent exclusive meaning "to sing," which it everywhere has in the New Testament. Hence, many of them constantly confuse the two meanings, and are consequently misleading on this point just as they are on baptism. They overlook the radical changes which the word underwent during its history. But there are others in this class equally eminent for scholarship who have not overlooked it, and their testimony is of great weight. We shall now hear what some of them of both classes have to say:

1. CONYBEARE AND HOWSON. Commenting on Eph. 5: 19, these eminent scholars of the Church of England say:

Throughout the whole passage there is a contrast implied between the heathen and the Christian practice, e. g. *when you meet, let your enjoyment consist* not in fullness of wine, but fullness of the Spirit; let your songs be, not the drinking songs of heathen feasts, but psalms and hymns; and their accompaniment, not the music of the lyre, but the melody of the heart; while you sing them to the praises not of

Bacchus or Venus, but of the Lord Jesus Christ.—
Life and Epistles of St. Paul, Vol. II., p. 408.

2. Joseph B. Mayor, Emeritus Professor of King's
College, London, commenting on James 5: 13, says:

Ψαλλέτω. Properly used of playing on a stringed
instrument, as Luc. Parasit. 17 οὔτε γὰρ αὐλεῖν ἔνι χωρὶς
αὐλῶν οὔτε ψάλλειν ἄνευ λύρας. We find it also used of
singing with the voice and with the heart, Eph. 5:
19, 1 Cor. 14: 15.—*Commentary on the Epistle of
James,* p. 162.

3. Bishop William Beveridge, "Lord Bishop of
St. Asaph," a very learned churchman who died in
the early part of the eighteenth century, and who was
styled "the great reviver and restorer of primitive
piety," is an important witness in the case. He favored the use of instrumental music in the worship;
but after a labored and unsuccessful effort to defend
it, he lays down a "rule" to be observed in its use,
and is compelled to say:

All the while that you are singing and praising
God, keep your minds as intent as you can upon it,
without taking any notice at all of the organs, for
they will have their effect upon you better if you do
not mind them than if you do; for your minding of
them will divert your thoughts from the work you
are about.—*Thesaurus Theologicus,* Vol. II., p. 523.

4. Charles Buck, English Independent minister,
referred to by the Schaff-Herzog Encyclopedia as

"the never-to-be-forgotten author of the Theological Dictionary,"—a work which still holds a place in the libraries of scholars, says:

Much has been said as to the use of instrumental music in the house of God. On the one side it is observed that we ought not to object to it, because it assists devotion; that it was used in the worship of God under the Old Testament; and that the worship of heaven is represented by a delightful union of vocal and instrumental music. But on the other side, it is remarked, that nothing should be done in or about God's worship without example or precept from the New Testament; that, instead of aiding devotion, it often tends to draw off the mind from the right object; that it does not accord with the simplicity of Christian worship; that the practice of those who lived under the ceremonial dispensation can be no rule for us; that not one text in the New Testament requires or authorizes it by precept or example, by express words or fair inference; and that the representation of the musical harmony in heaven is merely figurative language, denoting the happiness of the saints.—*Theological Dictionary, Art. Singing.*

5. ADAM CLARKE, the illustrious Methodist commentator, says:

But were it even evident, which it is not, either from this or any other place in the sacred writings, that instruments of music were prescribed by Divine authority *under the law,* could this be adduced with any semblance of reason, that they ought to be used in *Christian worship?* No; the whole spirit, soul, and genius of the Christian religion are against this: and those who know the Church of God best, and what *constitutes its genuine spiritual state,* know that these things have been introduced as a substitute for the *life* and *power* of religion; and that where they prevail most, there is least of the *power* of Christianity. Away with such portentous baubles from the worship of that infinite Spirit who requires his followers to worship him *in spirit and in truth,* for to no such worship are those instruments friendly.—*Commentary, Vol. II., pp.* 690, 691, *note on 2 Chron. 29: 25.*

Then, on Amos 6: 5, the same author says:

And invent to themselves instruments of music, like David]. See the note on 1 Chron. 23: 5; and especially the note on 2 Chron. 24: 25. I believe that David was not authorized by the Lord to introduce that multitude of musical instruments into the Divine worship of which we read; and I am satisfied that his conduct in this respect is most solemnly reprehended by the prophet; and I farther believe that the use of such instruments of music, in the Christian Church, is *without* the *sanction* and *against* the *will* of God; that they are subversive of the spirit of true devotion, and that they are *sinful.* If there was a *wo to them* who *invented* instruments of music, as did David under the law, is there *no wo, no curse* to them who invent them, and introduce them into the worship of God in the Christian Church? I am an old man, and an old minister; and I here declare that I never knew them productive of any good in the worship of God; and have had reason to believe that they were productive of much evil. Music, *as a science,* I esteem and admire: but instruments of music *in the house of God* I abominate and abhor. This is the abuse of music; and here I register my protest against all such corruptions in the worship of the Author of Christianity. The late venerable and most eminent divine, the Rev. *John Wesley*, who was a *lover of music*, and an *elegant poet*, when asked his opinion of instruments of music being introduced into the chapels of the Methodists, said in his terse and powerful manner, "I have no objection to instruments of music in our chapels, provided they are neither HEARD nor SEEN." I say the same, though I think the expense of purchase had better be spared.—*Commentary, Vol. IV. p. 686.*

6. MARVIN R. VINCENT, Baldwin Professor of Sacred Literature in Union Theological Seminary, New York—a Presbyterian of acknowledged scholarship, and the author of "Word Studies in the New Testament," commenting on 1 Cor. 14: 15, says:

I will sing (ψαλῶ). See on Jas. 5: 13. The verb ᾄδω is also used for *sing*, Eph. 5: 19; Col. 3: 16; Apoc. 5: 9; 14: 3; 15: 3. In the last two passages it is combined with playing on harps. In Eph. 5: 19 we have both verbs. The noun ψαλμός *psalm* (Eph. 5: 19; Col. 3: 16; 1 Cor. 14: 26), which is etymologically akin to this verb, is used in the New Testament of a religious song in general, having the character of an Old Testament psalm; though in Matt. 26: 30; Mark 14: 26, ὑμνέω *hymneo*, whence our *hymn*, is used of singing an Old Testament psalm. Here it is applied to such songs improvised under the spiritual ecstasy (ver. 26). Some think that the verb has here its original signification of singing with an instrument. This is its dominant sense in the Septuagint, and both Basil and Gregory of Nyssa define a psalm as implying instrumental accompaniment; and Clement of Alexandria, while forbidding the use of the flute in the agapæ, permitted the harp.* But neither Basil, nor Ambrose, nor Chrysostom, in their pane-gyrics upon music, mention instrumental music, and Basil expressly condemns it. Bingham dismisses the matter summarily, and cites Justin Martyr as say-ing expressly that instrumental music was not used in the Christian Church. The verb is used here in the general sense of singing praise.—*Word Studies, Vol. III., pp.* 269, 270.

7. Robert Milligan, who, for varied learning and scholarship particularly in theological and biblical lore, was practically unsurpassed at the time of his death in 1875, says:

The word *psalm* is from the Greek noun ψαλμός, and this again from the verb ψάλλω, to touch, to feel, to play on a stringed instrument with the fingers, and, finally, to make music or melody in the heart, as in Eph. 5: 19. The meaning of the noun corresponds with that of the verb, and denotes a touching, a play-ing on a stringed instrument, any song or ode. And hence it is evident that the word *psalm* may or may not refer to instrumental music. Its proper mean-ing, in any and every case, must be determined by the context. And, according to this fundamental law of interpretation, it is pretty evident that in Ephe-sians and Colossians the term ψαλμός has no reference to instrumental music; for, in both cases, it is the

---

*The Greek of Clement does not necessarily mean this. For a discussion of the point, see Chap. XII., page 124 of this work.

strings or chords of the heart, and not of an instrument, that are to be touched.

Then, in reply to the question whether instrumental music should be used in Christian worship, he gives a negative answer with five reasons for it, as follows:

(1). Such a practice is wholly unwarranted by anything that is either said or taught in the New Testament. The inspired Psalmist said to his Jewish brethren,

"Praise him (Jehovah) with the sound of the trumpet;
Praise him with the psaltery and harp;
Praise him with the timbrel and dance;
Praise him with stringed instruments and organs;
Praise him on the loud cymbals;
Praise him on the high-sounding cymbals."
—Psa. 150: 3-5.

But Paul says to all Christians, "Teach and admonish one another in Psalms, and Hymns, and Spiritual Songs, singing and making melody (ψάλλοντες, *psalming*) in your hearts to the Lord." Eph. 5: 19. The antithesis here is certainly very marked, and seems to be intentional and significant.

(2). It is at least doubtful whether such a practice is in harmony with the tenor and spirit of the Christian Institution.

(3). The tendency of instrumental music is, I think, to divert the minds of many from the sentiment of the song to the mere sound of the organ, and in this way it often serves to promote formalism in Churches.

(4). I am not aware that instrumental music has ever served to promote unity, peace, harmony, and love in any congregation of Christians; but I am aware that in some of them it has had a contrary effect.

(5). It is often at variance with the law of love.—*Scheme of Redemption*, pp. 380-387.

8. Expositor's Greek Testament:

Ψάλλω denoted, first, *playing on strings*, then *singing* to such accompaniment; Eph. 5: 19 distinguishes this verb from ᾄδω. Ed. thinks that instrumentation is implied; unless forbidden, Gr. Christians would be sure to grace their songs with music. Through its Lxx. use, especially in the title ψαλμοί, t'hillim (Heb.), the word came to signify *the singing of praise to God.—On 1 Cor. 14: 15.*

9. Charles John Ellicott, the eminent "Bishop of Gloucester and Bristol," mentioned sometimes by way of preëminence as the De Wette of English commentators, says on Eph. 5: 19:

"With psalms and hymns and spiritual songs." The distinctions between these words have been somewhat differently estimated. Olshausen and Stier would confine ψαλμὸs to the Psalms of the Old Testament, ὕμνος to any Christian song of praise; this does not seem borne out by 1 Cor. 14: 26, compare Jas. 5: 13. * * * In a passage so general as the present, no such rigorous distinctions seem called for; ψαλμὸs most probably, as Meyer suggests, denotes a sacred song of a character similar to that of the Psalms, * * *; ὕμνος, a song more especially of

praise, whether to Christ (ver. 19), or God (ver. 20; compare Acts 16: 25, Heb. 2: 12); ᾠδή, a definition generally of the genus to which all such compositions belonged. * * * ᾄδοντες καὶ ψάλλοντες] *"singing and making melody in your heart;"* participal clause, *co-ordinate with* (Meyer), not *subordinate to* (so as to specify the moral quality of the psalmody, μετὰ συνέσεως, Chrysostom) the foregoing λαλοῦντες, etc. Harless very clearly shows that ἐν τῇ καρδιᾳ, without ὑμῶν, could not indicate any antithesis between the heart and lips, much less any qualitative definition,— * * * but that simply *another* kind of psalmody is mentioned, that of the inward heart.

Thus, this eminent New Testament exegete carefully distinguishes between the melody made, as in the ancient usage of ψάλλω, on the lyre or other instrument, and that made, in the New Testament usage of the term, in the heart. The latter is so distinct from the former that he calls it *"another* kind of psalmody."

Then, he translates and comments on 1 Cor. 14: 15 as follows:

"I will sing praise with the spirit, and I will sing praise with the understanding;" i. e. "I will not only sing praise with my spirit, but will interpret what I sing." The term ψάλλειν (properly τὸ διὰ δακτύλων ἐπὶ ψαύειν τῶν χόρδων τῆς λύρας, *Etym. M.*) is here probably used without any reference to any instrument (Comp. Jas. 5: 13), but as denoting the singing of *praise*.

Thus, this eminent critic finds the instrument ruled out of this passage; and on strong contextual and

186

philological grounds, many eminent scholars, some of whom are quoted in this work, find it ruled out of every other passage containing the word whether in the New Testament or in cotemporaneous literature.

10. HEINRICH AUGUST WILHELM MEYER, the eminent Lutheran scholar and New Testament commentator, referred to by competent critics as the "prince of exegetes," makes the following comment on Eph. 5: 19:

The distinction between ψαλμός and ὕμνος consists in this, that by ψαλμός Paul denotes *a religious song in general bearing the character of the Old Testament psalms*, but by ὕμνος specially a *song of praise,* and that, in accordance with the context, addressed to Christ (ver. 19) and God (ver. 20). Properly ψαλμός (which originally means the making the cithara sound) is a song in general, and that indeed as sung to a stringed instrument; but in the New Testament the character of the psalm is determined by the psalms of the Old Testament, so called κατ' ἐξοχήν, "preëminently" (1 Cor. 14: 15, 26; Jas. 5: 13). According to Harless, the two words are not different as regards their contents, but ψαλμοῖς is the expression of the spiritual song for the *Jewish-Christians,* ὕμνοις for the *Gentile-Christians.* An external distinction in itself improbable, and very arbitrary, since the special signification of ὕμνος, *song of praise,* is thoroughly established, and ψαλμός also was a word very current in Greek, which—as well in itself as more especially with regard to its sense established in Christian usage in accordance with the conception of the Old Testament psalms—could not but be equally intelligible for the Gentile-Christians as for the Jewish-Christians. According to Olshausen, ψαλμοί are here the *psalms of the Old Testament*, which had passed over from the synagogue into the use of the church. But worship is not spoken of here; and that the Christians, filled by the Spirit, *improvised* psalms, is clear from 1 Cor. 14: 15, 26. Such *Christian* psalms and hymns are meant, as the Spirit gave them to be uttered (Acts 2: 4, 10: 46, 19: 6),—phenomena doubtless, which, like the operations of the Spirit generally in the first age of the church, are withdrawn from our special cognizance. —καὶ ᾠδαῖς πνευματικαῖς.] Inasmuch as ᾠδή may be any song, even secular, πνευματικαῖς is here added, so that by ᾠδαῖς πνευματικαῖς is denoted the whole *genus*, of which the ψαλμοί and ὕμνοι were *species*. * * * ᾄδοντες καὶ ψάλλοντες ἐν τῇ καρδίᾳ ὑμῶν τῷ κυρίῳ] coördinate with the preceding λαλοῦντες κ. τ. λ. containing *another* singing of praise, namely, that which goes on *in the silence of the heart*. The point of difference lies in ἐν ταῖς καρδίαις ὑμῶν, as contradistinguished from the preceding ἑαυτοῖς. *Usually* this second participial clause is regarded as *subordinate* to the previous one; it is held to affirm that that reciprocal singing of praise must take place not merely with the mouth, but also in the heart. But how could it have occurred to Paul here to enter such a protest against mere lip-praise, when he, in fact, represents the psalm-singing, etc., as the utterance of the being filled by the Spirit, and makes express mention of πνευματικαῖς ᾠδαῖς, in which case, at any rate, the thought of a mere singing with the mouth was of itself excluded.—*Commentary on the New Testament*, Gal. and Eph., pp. 506, 507.

Now, notwithstanding this eminent authority favored instrumental music in the worship, and while he does not say, in specific terms, that this idea had disappeared from ψάλλω in its New Testament usage, yet the testimony which he bears clearly shows that he recognized a change of meaning in the word at the opening of the New Testament period. In proof of this, we collate and submit the following facts candidly admitted by him in the passage quoted:

1. He says ψαλμός "originally means the making the cithara sound." Mark the word "originally." In Chapter II., of the present work, which is devoted to the Lexicons, it is abundantly shown that this was one of its ancient meanings—a fact freely conceded by those who deny that it had this meaning in New Testament times.

2. Although he says it "properly" means "a song in general, and that indeed as sung to a stringed instrument," yet it is clear that, in his case, as in that of many other scholars, its ancient classical meaning is confused with its later meaning. This is shown by his use of different expressions which seem to be intended to make the impression that there is some sort of *difference* in the meaning of the term in the two periods. For instance, referring to ψαλμός as "a word very current in Greek," he speaks particularly of "its sense established in Christian usage," which he would hardly do if, in his judgment, that usage did not vary from classical usage.

3. He testifies that in Eph. 5: 19, where the "*psalloing*" is said to be "in the heart," and where the word is used in connection with ᾅδω, another word meaning to sing, it denotes "*another* singing of

praise, namely, that which goes on *in the silence of the heart."*

4. Finally, he describes all the music of the passage signified by ψάλλω as "psalm-*singing*," and this cannot mean psalm-playing.

11. Erasmus (Desiderius), a cotemporary of Martin Luther, who has the reputation of being the most renowned classical scholar of his age and is represented by high authority as "the most gifted and industrious pioneer of modern scholarship," says:

We have brought into our churches a certain operose and theatrical music; such a confused, disorderly chattering of some words, as I hardly think was ever heard in any of the Grecian or Roman theatres. The church rings with the noise of trumpets, pipes and dulcimers; and human voices strive to bear their part with them. * * * Men run to church as to a theatre, to have their ears tickled. And for this end organ-makers are hired with great salaries, and a company of boys, who waste all their time in learning these whining tones.—*Commentary on* 1 Cor. 14: 19.

12. John Calvin. This illustrious Reformer and reputed founder of Presbyterianism says:

Musical instruments in celebrating the praises of God would be no more suitable than the burning of incense, the lighting up of lamps, and the restoration of the other shadows of the law. The papists, therefore, have foolishly borrowed this, as well as many other things, from the Jews. Men who are fond of outward pomp may delight in that noise; but the simplicity which God recommends to us by the apostle is far more pleasing to Him. Paul allows us to bless God in the public assembly of the saints, only in a known tongue (1 Cor. 14: 16). The voice of man, although not understood by the generality, assuredly excels all inanimate instruments of music; and yet we see what Paul determines concerning speaking in an unknown tongue. What shall we then say of chanting which fills the ears with nothing but an empty sound? * * * What, therefore, was in use under the law is by no means entitled to our practice under the Gospel; and these things being not only superfluous, but useless, are to be abstained from because pure and simple modulation is sufficient for the praise of God, if it is sung with the heart and with the mouth. We know that our Lord Jesus Christ has appeared, and by His advent has abolished these legal shadows. Instrumental music, we therefore maintain, was only tolerated on account of the times and the people, because they were as boys, as the sacred Scripture speaketh, whose condition required these puerile rudiments. But in gospel times we must not have recourse to these unless we wish to destroy the evangelical perfection and to obscure the meridian light which we enjoy in Christ our Lord.—*Calvin's Commentary on the Thirty-third Psalm, and on 1 Sam. 18: 1-9.*

13. JOHN CHRYSOSTOM. This celebrated Greek Father of the church, whose Homilies on the Scriptures have been widely circulated, lived in the fourth century of the Christian era, being born, as noted on a preceding page, A.D. 347. His period, therefore, extends back to within two hundred and fifty years

of the Apostles, and even at that early day the same view which, as we have seen, was advocated by Calvin, was held as to why instrumental music was allowed in the Jewish worship. Chrysostom says:

It was only permitted to the Jews as sacrifice was, for the heaviness and grossness of their souls. God condescended to their weakness, because they were lately drawn off from idols; but now, instead of organs, we may use our own bodies to praise him withal.—*Chrysostom on Psa.* 149, *Vol.* iii. *p.* 634, Paris, 1616; and *on Psa.* 144, *Vol.* i. *p.* 862, cited by *Bingham, Vol. II., p.* 485, London Edit.*

14. JUSTIN MARTYR. Wherever Christianity has been long established, the name of this justly celebrated Church Father of Palestine, who is said to have suffered martyrdom in the year 165, is well known. He was born at the beginning of the second

---

*The following is the Greek of the two passages: On Psa. 149—
Τὰ ὄργανα δὲ ἐκεῖνα διὰ τοῦτο ἐπιτέτραπτο τότε, διάτε τὴν ἀσθένειαν αὐτῶν, καὶ διὰ τὸ κιρνᾷν αὐτοὺς εἰς ἀγάπην καὶ συμφωνίαν καὶ ἐγείρειν αὐτῶν τὴν διάνοιαν μεθ' ἡδονῆς ποιεῖν τὰ τὴν ὠφέλειαν παρεχόμενα, καὶ εἰς πολλὴν βούλεσθαι αὐτοὺς ἄγειν σπουδὴν διὰ τῆς τοιαύτης ψυχαγωγιας· τὸ γὰρ βάναυσον αὐτῶν καὶ ῥᾴθυμον καὶ ἀναπεπτωκὸς σοφιζόμενος ὁ θεὸς, ἀφυπνίζειν αὐτοὺς ταύτῃ μεθώδευσε τῇ σοφίᾳ, ἀνακεράσας τῷ πόνῳ τῆς προσεδρίας τὸ ἡδὺ τῆς μελῳδίας.

Ibid. on Psa. 144—Τότε μὲν ὄργανα ἦν, δι' ὧν τὰς ᾠδὰς ἀνέφερον· νυνὶ δὲ ἀντὶ ὀργάνων κεχρῆσθαί ἐστι τῷ σώματι· ἔστι γὰρ καὶ δι' ὀφθαλμῶν ᾄδειν, οὐ διὰ γλώττης μόνον, καὶ διὰ χειρῶν, καὶ διὰ ποδῶν, καὶ ἀκοῆς. Ὅταν γὰρ ἕκαστον τούτων ταῦτα πράττῃ, ἃ τῷ θεῷ φέρει δόξαν καὶ αἶνον, οἷον, ἂν μὴ ἀκόλαστα ὀφθαλμὸς βλέπῃ, ὅταν μὴ πρὸς ἁρπαγὰς αἱ χεῖρες, ἀλλὰ πρὸς ἐλεημοσύνην ὦσι τεταμέναι, ὅταν πρὸς ψαλμῶν καὶ πνευματικῶν ἀκουσμάτων ὑποδοχὴν αἱ ἀκοαὶ παρασκευασμέναι· ὅταν πρὸς ἐκκλησίαν οἱ πόδες τρέχωσιν, ὅταν ἡ καρδία δόλους μὴ ῥάπτῃ, ἀλλ' ἀγάπην βρύῃ, γίνεται ψαλτήριον καὶ κιθάρα τοῦ σώματος τὰ μέλη, καὶ ᾄδει καινὴν ᾠδήν, οὐ τὴν διὰ ῥημάτων, ἀλλὰ τὴν διὰ πραγμάτων.

century, and hence his period begins where the apostolic period closed. His testimony is, therefore, of the greatest importance that can be justly attached to the testimony of uninspired men. Eusebius says (Book IV. Chap. 11.) that he "was the most noted of those that flourished in" the second century. We quote him among the commentators that his testimony may be considered in connection with that of Chrysostom and Calvin in its bearing on the question of instrumental music in the Jewish worship as well as in Christian worship.

A considerable number of Justin's writings have come down to us, and some have been attributed to him, concerning the genuineness of which, scholars are not agreed. The work entitled, "QUESTIONS AND ANSWERS TO THE ORTHODOX," which has long been attributed to him, is claimed by some critics to have been written by another person. But even if it were proven conclusively that Justin was not the author of this work, it remains a fact that it was written by some Christian scholar of that early period, or near that period, and its testimony, even in such an event, would still be of the greatest value. On the subject which we now have in hand, this ancient author, as we render his language, says:

Simply singing is not agreeable to children, but singing with lifeless instruments and with dancing and clapping; on which account the use of this kind of instruments and of others agreeable to children is removed from the songs in the churches, and there is left remaining simply singing.—*Justin's Questions and Answers to the Orthodox*, Ques. 107, p. 462.*

This testimony is certainly explicit and to the point. The term which he uses for children (νήπιοι) is the same used by Paul in Gal. 4: 1, 3, and the context shows that he intends to describe by it the infant state of the Jews under the law, and that it was because of this undeveloped condition that the Lord permitted the use of instrumental music in the Jewish worship. Be this as it may, he is very clear and positive as to its omission from the worship after the establishment of the church.

15. THEODORE BEZA, the great Genevan scholar and translator, who was a friend and coadjutor of Calvin, says:

If the apostle justly prohibits the use of unknown tongues in the church, much less would he have tolerated these artificial musical performances which are addressed to the ear alone, and seldom strike the understanding even of the performers themselves.—*Girardeau's Instrumental Music*, p. 166.

16. DAVID PAREUS, a scholar of the seventeenth century and a Professor of theology in the Heidelberg University, says:

---

*The Greek of the passage is as follows: Οὐ τὸ ᾆσαι ἁπλῶς ἐστι τοῖς νηπίοις ἁρμόδιον, ἀλλὰ τὸ μετὰ τῶν ἀψύχων ὀργάνων ᾆσαι, καὶ μετὰ ὀρχήσεως καὶ κροτάλων· διὸ ἐν ταῖς ἐκκλησίαις προαίρεται ἐκ τῶν ᾀσμάτων ἡ χρῆσις τῶν τοιούτων ὀργάνων, καὶ τῶν ἄλλων τῶν νηπίοις ὄντων ἁρμοδίων, καὶ ὑπολέλειπται τὸ ᾆσαι ἁπλῶς.—Justin. Quaest. 107.

In the Christian church the mind must be incited to spiritual joy, not by pipes and trumpets and timbrels, with which God formerly indulged his ancient people on account of the hardness of their hearts, but by psalms and hymns and spiritual songs.—*Commentary on* 1 Cor. 14: 7.

17. Dean Henry Alford. This brilliant commentator on the Greek New Testament, though strongly in favor of instrumental music in the worship, yet is compelled, as a scholar, to make statements which support the opposition, renders *psalleto* (ψαλλέτω) in Jas. 5: 13—"let him sing praise." He then adds in parenthesis the significant remarks:

Literally play on an instrument; but used in reff. Rom. and 1 Cor. and elsewhere of singing praise generally. The word *"Psalm"* is an evidence of this latter sense.

Then, on Eph. 5: 19, he renders the words ᾄδοντες καὶ ψάλλοντες ἐν τῇ καρδίᾳ ὑμῶν, "singing and playing in your hearts." The playing, according to Alford, is in the heart. On the term ψαλμός in this passage, he says:

The word properly signifies those sacred songs which were performed with musical accompaniment, as ὕμνοι without it; but the two must evidently here not be confined strictly to their proper meaning.

According to these candid utterances, this great New Testament exegete knew that the word *psallo* (ψάλλω) in the New Testament meant to sing, and was used as meaning to play, only in a figurative sense; that is, *to play in the heart.*

195

On *psalmos* (ψαλμός) in 1 Cor. 14: 26 he says:

Most probably a hymn of praise to sing in the power of the Spirit, as did Miriam, Deborah, Simeon, etc.

18. Charles Haddon Spurgeon. It is a well-known fact that this renowned London preacher, whose name is familiar in religious circles throughout the English-speaking world, did not use instrumental music in the worship. In the Metropolitan Tabernacle, London, where thousands gathered every week to hear him preach, simply singing without any kind of instrumental music, was used. James A. Garfield, after attending worship in the famous Tabernacle and listening to the mighty volume of vocal melody that went up in praise to God, said, on his return to the United States, that for once in his life, while listening to that impressive service of song, he had sympathy with those who did not use instrumental music in the worship. Of this distinguished preacher some time before his death, Professor Girardeau said:

Some few yet stand firm against what is now called, in a painfully significant phrase, the ''down-grade'' tendencies of this age. Prominent among them is that eminent servant of Christ—a star in His right hand—the Rev. Charles H. Spurgeon, who not only proclaims with power the pure doctrines of God's word, but retains and upholds an apostolic simplicity of worship. The great congregation which

196

is blessed with the privilege of listening to his instructions has no organ "to assist" them in singing their praises to their God and Savior. They find their vocal organs sufficient. Their tongues and voices express the gratitude of their hearts.—*Instrumental Music in the Church*, p. 176.

CHAPTER XV.

Testimony of Leading Scholars Connected with the Religious Restoration of the Nineteenth Century.

In all the literature produced by the inaugurators and propagators of the religious Restoration of the nineteenth century, which originated with Barton W. Stone and the two Campbells—Thomas and Alexander, no fact, perhaps, stands out with greater prominence or clearness than the distinction definitely drawn by them between *faith* and *opinion*. They drew the line broad and deep, and then insisted, with great earnestness and emphasis, that this line must be constantly and strictly observed by all who would restore the ancient order in doctrine and in life. Moreover, they insisted, with equal earnestness and emphasis, that all matters on the side of opinion, except such as are "indispensably necessary to the observance of Divine ordinances," must be held as "private property" without ever "publishing or practicing" them "so as to give offense" to others.

Now, if it be possible to settle any fact by clear, explicit, and positive statement repeated over and over again, then these two facts are clearly and in-

controvertibly settled. Furthermore, so far as the
first of these facts is concerned, viz., that the reformers referred to divided matters pertaining to religion into these two classes—*matters of opinion* and
matters of faith—there is practically universal
agreement to-day; but with reference to the *second*
fact, viz., that opinions must be held as "private
property" to the full extent of never "publishing or
practicing" them "so as to give offense" to others,
or in any way cause trouble in the church, there has
been a growing tendency for a long time, and it is
still spreading and strengthening itself, to ignore
this fundamental point in the plea of the reformers,
and to represent them as occupying a position in
regard to this matter which they never occupied.
Touching the matters belonging on the opinion side
of the line, we are told that the "fathers" of this
Restoration contended for the "largest liberty;"
that in matters of faith they were unyielding, but
in matters of opinion they allowed the largest liberty. Thus far, we here freely admit, the representation of the "fathers" is correct. They did allow the *largest liberty* in the mere matter of holding opinions; but just here is the point at which the
mistake and the misrepresentation begin. While
the "fathers" allowed the largest liberty in holding
opinions, they not only did not teach that the mere
liberty to hold an opinion carried with it the liberty
to teach or practice it, but they taught, in the clearest and strongest terms, the very opposite of this,

and insisted that in all cases, opinions, with the one exception before noted, must be held in "private" without ever "publishing or practicing" them "so as to give offense" to others or cause strife and division in the church.

Hence, with all due respect to those who have given, and are still giving, impetus to this tendency, we here unhesitatingly affirm that whoever urges, or in any way countenances, the *practice of an opinion* in a church in a case in which, like the use of instrumental music in the worship, a part of the membership are opposed to the practice and have to refrain from it in order to preserve a pure conscience, violates the plea of the "fathers" by making the identical use of opinion which *they prohibited in the strongest possible terms.*

In order that we may set this matter in its true light, we now appeal directly to the "fathers" of this Restoration themselves, that the reader may see, from their own words, both their *theory* and their *practice* on matters of opinion in religion.

I. Theory of the "Fathers" on Opinions.

1. Barton Warren Stone. We place this amiable and illustrious man at the head of the list because, both in priority of time and in the formidable and embarrassing opposition which he encountered and overcame, if not in intellectuality and breadth of learning, he is indeed, if not *the* first (*primus inter pares*) at least among the first reformers of the

nineteenth century. He was sixteen years the senior of Alexander Campbell, and the great plea for the union of Christians upon the Bible alone was in full blast in parts of Kentucky under the leadership of Barton W. Stone when Alexander Campbell was a youth of seventeen years assisting his father in the work of teaching in the academy at Rich Hill, Ireland. In an Address "To the Church Scattered throughout America," in an admirable passage on union in which he shows how opinions must be kept in private and never made the occasion of contention and division among brethren, this pious reformer said:

We may be so captivated by the doctrines, forms, popularity, and respectability of the sects around us that we may try to accommodate the truth of God to their prejudices, in order to gain their favor, and eventually to enlist them on our side, and join in our mighty union. Such union is no better than, if as good as, that of the Romanists, who are exceedingly jealous for union. A union of ten pious, uncompromising persons in the truth, is better than ten thousand of the contrary character. Truth must never be sacrificed for the union of numbers. Truth preached and lived in the spirit will cut its way through all opposition. But what is truth? The Bible, and the Bible alone—not opinions which men have formed of the Bible, whether comprised in a confession of faith, a Christian system, or in thirty-nine articles, or in a discipline. Our union first commenced on this ground, and sectarianism first received its deadly wound from this weapon, and by no other will it die the death, if its death is to be effected by moral means. If we begin to magnify our opinions, and make them tests of fellowship, we depart from the foundation laid in Zion, and shall be under the necessity of becoming a sect by forming a book of opinions as our creed and demanding a subscription to it as the basis of union.—*Pioneer Sermons and Addresses,* pp. 150, 151.

Of this pious reformer and his plea for Christian union, his gifted biographer, John Rogers, says:

Of all the subjects relating to the interests of the church of God, that of the union of Christians on Heaven's own terms, was dearest and nearest to the heart of the pious Stone. Most sincerely, most industriously, most consistently, and most successfully did he advocate this doctrine for forty years.—*Biography of B. W. Stone,* p. 317.

2. Thomas and Alexander Campbell. That the reader may see the position held and advocated by these two great reformers, we here introduce some passages from the famous "Declaration and Address:"

(1) Our differences, at most, are about the things in which the Kingdom of God does not consist, that is, about matters of private opinion or human invention. What a pity that the Kingdom of God should be divided about such things! Who, then, would not be the first among us to give up human inventions in the worship of God, and to cease from imposing his private opinions upon his brethren, that our breaches might *thus* be healed?

202

(2) Nothing ought to be inculcated upon Christians as articles of faith, nor required of them as terms of communion, but what is expressly taught and enjoined upon them in the word of God.

(3) If any circumstantials indisputably necessary to the observance of Divine ordinances be not found upon the page of express revelation, such, and such only, as are absolutely necessary for this purpose should be adopted under the title of human expedients, . . . so that any subsequent alteration or difference in the observance of these things might produce no contention nor division in the church.

(4) We dare not, therefore, patronize the rejection of God's dear children because they may not be able to see alike in matters of human inference—of private opinion; and such we esteem all things not expressly revealed and enjoined in the word of God.

(5) According to the principle adopted, we can neither take offense at our brother for his private opinions, if he be content to hold them as such, nor yet offend him with ours, if he do not usurp the place of lawgiver; and even suppose he should, in this case we judge him, not for his *opinions,* but for his presumption.

(6) No man can relinquish his opinions or practices till once convinced that they are wrong; and this he may not be immediately, even supposing they were so. One thing, however, he may do: when not bound by an express command, he need not impose them upon others, by anywise requiring their approbation; and when this is done, the things, to them, are as good as dead, yea, as good as buried, too, being thus removed out of the way.

(7) And here let it be noted, that it is not the renunciation of an opinion or practice as sinful that

203

is proposed or intended, but merely a cessation from the publishing or practicing it, so as to give offense; a thing men are in the habit of doing every day for their private comfort or secular emolument, where the advantage is of infinitely less importance. Neither is there here any clashing of duties, as if to forbear was a sin and also to practice was sin; the thing to be forborne being a matter of private opinion, which, though not expressly forbidden, yet are we by no means expressly commanded to practice; whereas we are expressly commanded to endeavor to maintain the unity of the Spirit in the bond of peace.—*Memoirs of Thomas Campbell, pp.* 39, 48, 49, 52, 64, 66, 68, 69, 70.

3. J. T. Johnson. In a letter to Alexander Campbell concerning the union of the so-called Reformers and Christians led, respectively, by Campbell and Stone, this eminent evangelist makes the following observation on opinions:

The union was based upon the Bible and the terms therein contained—a union of brethren who were contending for the facts, truths, commands, and promises as set forth in the divinely inspired record, the Bible alone; with the express understanding that opinions and speculations were private property—no part of the faith delivered to the saints, and that such matters should never be debated to the annoyance and to the disturbance of the peace and harmony of the brotherhood.—*Biography of B. W. Stone,* p. 346.

4. John Smith. In an "Address" concerning this same union, which had been effected between

the Christians and the Reformers, written mainly because of certain misapprehensions entertained by the latter, this venerable preacher who blazed much of the way for Reformation in his day, makes this pointed and interesting statement on our theme:

It may be asked, if the people called *Christians,* who have ceased to speculate upon the character of Christ, have given up their Unitarian opinions? And may it not as well be asked, have they who speculate upon the character of Christ before they become Reformers, given up their Trinitarian opinions? To both these questions I would answer, I do not know, neither do I care. We should always allow to others that which we claim for ourselves— *the right of private judgment.* If either Christians or Reformers have erroneous opinions, they never can injure any person, provided we all have prudence enough to keep them to ourselves. Neither will they injure us if we continue to believe the Gospel facts and obey the law of the King. If all who profess to be teachers of the Christian religion would keep their opinions to themselves, teach the Gospel facts, and urge the people to obey them, the world would soon be delivered from the wretched, distracting, and destructive influences of mystical preaching.—*Life of Elder John Smith,* p. 468.

5. PRESIDENT JAMES SHANNON. This distinguished and scholarly man, who was President of the College of Louisiana in 1838, testifies as follows:

I have never yet found a single advocate of human creeds (not even the most talented) who did not confound *faith* with *opinion,* although the two ideas are as perfectly distinct from each other as *horse* and *house.* . . . *Faith* consists in receiving testimony as true, and is but one degree removed from the certainty of knowledge. . . . *Opinion,* on the other hand, is merely an inference which the mind draws from premises that are at best but probable. In our opinions, therefore, there is room for every possible degree of uncertainty and liability to error. . . . To have made agreement in opinions a bond of Union among Christians would have rendered that Union impossible, and would inevitably have rent the body of Christ into as many factions and sects as are the diversified opinions to which minds equally honest and independent may be led by the investigation of the same subjects. . . . But, says one, it is unreasonable to expect that men would give up their opinions; and consequently they cannot unite in one body. This is a genuine sophism. It takes it for granted that Christians cannot unite without abandoning their opinions; whereas nothing more is necessary than that they should *not impose them on others* as a condition of membership.—*The Christian Preacher,* July, 1838.

6. TOLBERT F A N N I N G. This intellectual giant among those pleading for reformation and union, says:

Our great and distinguished men, long since, lost all hope of unity in opinion, and hence, they abandoned religious opinions and soon reached the conclusion that all "who believe, through the words of the Spirit, are one in faith." Never, till we can satisfy the world that there is but one faith, and that it comes through the hearing of the word of God, can we make ourselves very successful in turning men from darkness to light, and from the power of Satan to God. All men, however, who look up to God through the same medium can but see eye to eye and speak the same things. If we differ, then, it is because of ignorance of the truth. This rule is universal in its application. Let us endeavor to adhere to it in all our investigations.—*Gospel Advocate, November* 19, 1868, p. 2012.

The list of witnesses on this particular phase of the subject might be extended, but these are sufficient for our present purpose. Summing up the testimony of these distinguished men, we find that the "fathers" accepted the following items as settled facts:

1. That, in order to stop strife and division in the church, every Christian ought to be willing "to give up . . . his private opinions" to the extent of ceasing "from imposing" them upon others.

2. That, in observing divine ordinances, no "human expedient" should be adopted except such as will "produce no contention nor division in the church."

3. The right to have different opinions is clearly guaranteed to Christians in the word of God, and we must, therefore, not reject any of God's children merely because they do not "see alike in matters of . . . private opinion."

4. If our brother "be content to hold" his opin-

ions in "private" on any subject, we cannot take offense at him, nor can we offend him with ours.

5. "One thing, however," we must guard, namely, "when not bound by an express command," we must not impose our opinions "upon others," and then such opinions, so far as other persons are concerned, are as good as dead and buried, "being thus removed out of the way."

6. "It is not the renunciation of an opinion or practice as sinful that is proposed, but merely a cessation from publishing or practicing it so as to give offense."

7. Finally, all opinions, the advocacy or practice of which is attended with strife and division among brethren, must be held in private, not on the ground that they are "expressly forbidden," but on the ground that we are not only not "commanded to practice" them, but "we are expressly commanded to endeavor to maintain the unity of the Spirit in the bond of peace."

Now, in the light of these seven facts, who cannot see that the "fathers," although freely and explicitly allowing to Christians the right to hold opinions on any subject, and even different and conflicting opinions on the same subject, yet they taught, in the clearest and most explicit terms, that all opinions, whose practice brings strife and division, must be held in private? The case is too clear to admit of doubt, and we are content to leave it to the decision of candid and unbiased readers.

II. Practice of the "Fathers" on Opinions.

We are now prepared to see whether the "fathers" carried out in practice what we have seen they so clearly taught in theory. To reduce our investigation to something tangible, did their practice on the mooted question of instrumental music in the worship harmonize with their general theory about opinions in religion? It is universally conceded—at least the concession is so nearly universal as to make it unnecessary to mention exceptions—that this practice rests exclusively on human opinion, and not on any "Thus saith the Lord" making it obligatory upon the churches. Now, in view of this concession, and in view of the fact that the practice has been attended with strife and division from its very first introduction by the Romish hierarchy down to this hour, did the "fathers" of this Restoration movement refrain from this practice in order that they might stand on common ground and thus preserve peace and harmony in the church? We now propose to show that they did, and that the leading scholars among their successors, both the dead and the living, have taught the same thing.

The reader should remember that in the early days of the Restoration, the brethren everywhere were so thoroughly united against this and all other divisive opinions in religion, that it scarcely ever came up for debate, or even for reference; and hence, although their uniform *practice* everywhere, without exception, was against it, yet they seldom had occasion to express themselves on the subject, which accounts for the fact that, from some of them, we have no expression at all. However, those who did express themselves leave no room for doubt that they all stood as a solid unit against the practice. We now call upon this distinguished roll of reformers with their associates and successors to speak for themselves:

1. ALEXANDER CAMPBELL. This great scholar and reformer, who justly stands at the head of this list, says:

To those who have no real devotion or spirituality in them, and whose animal nature flags under the oppression of church service, I think that instrumental music would be not only a desideratum, but an essential prerequisite to fire up their souls to even animal devotion. But I presume to all spiritually-minded Christians, such aids would be as a cow bell in a concert.—*Memoirs of A. Campbell*, p. 366.

2. SAMUEL ROGERS. This great servant of God, who was only one year the junior of Alexander Campbell, describing the pioneer times, says:

It must be remembered that almost every convert we made in those days was required to pray, not only at home, but in the church also; and all who had voices to sing, sung with the spirit; whether with the understanding or not, I will not venture to say. We had no choirs then to do the singing for the congregation, and we certainly had no organs—not even a tuning fork.—*Autobiography*, p. 71.

3. THOMAS M. ALLEN. That the reader may know something of the high character of this eminent man of God, we add here, before submitting his testimony, the following estimate of his talents and standing as found in the Autobiography of Samuel Rogers:

T. M. Allen was Missouri's model evangelist and pioneer preacher. Having talents of a high order, a liberal education, refined manners, and a commanding appearance, with the Gospel at his tongue's end, it is not strange that he became at once the model and teacher of so many young men of that region. I have heard it said that he could put more Bible truth into a single sermon than any man west of the Mississippi.—P. 187.

This gifted gospel preacher, writing after the spirit of innovation had already entered the Reformation and begun, on a small scale, its deadly work, says:

Since I have been writing these numbers I have been thrown back to the early days of my ministerial career. It has given me great pleasure to mingle in memory with the noble sisters and brethren who then bore such a noble part in this glorious movement. They who live now know but little of the difficulties we had to meet and overcome. They now have their fine meetinghouses. We had the courthouse, private residences, and groves to worship in and under. We had but few friends, and were opposed by all religionists. We are now strong, and the unprejudiced mind has decreed in our favor. We succeeded by the truth, the pure Gospel of Jesus Christ, and after having triumphed by its power, what a burning shame it is that some of our congregations have made *shipwreck* of faith and apostatized *by aping* the sects, and going into the embrace of the mother of harlots by substituting *organ-grinding* for the worship of God, which must be in spirit and truth. * * * I thank the Lord that none of the congregations that I was instrumental in organizing have become *organ-grinders.—Apostolic Times,* March 10, 1870, p. 377.

4. ROBERT MILLIGAN. This truly great and learned man, who was not only a man of profound and varied scholarship, but who was probably one of the most distinguished examples of personal piety and goodness that ever lived, has already been quoted at length in this work in Chapter XIV. The reader is referred to the list of commentators quoted in that Chapter where, with other good things on the subject from this pious and learned man, will be found his declaration that the use of instrumental music in Christian worship "is wholly unwarranted by anything that is either said or taught in the New Testament."

5. PHILIP S. FALL. From this veteran pioneer preacher and teacher, we have the following strong testimony. Writing on the significant subject, "An

Organ in Every Congregation of Our Lord Jesus Christ," he says:

"No man cometh unto the Father but by—that is through, ME." A mediator, then, is a *sine qua non* to any approach to God; and he that comes must have made that mediator his mediator by accepting him as Lord and Christ, and putting him on. "Through him let us offer up a sacrifice of praise to God continually, that is the fruit of our lips, which make confession to his name." * * * "I will declare thy name unto my brethren, in the midst of the congregation will I sing praises unto thee." Psa. 22: 22; Heb. 2: 12. Here is a prophecy, uttered a thousand years before the Pentecost of A.D. 30, in which the Christ, by the mouth of David, represents himself as really taking part in the worship of his brethren; that is, of such as wear the name of their elder brother. Another remarkable passage teaches this also: "I will not drink, henceforth, of this fruit of the vine, until the day when I drink it new with you in my Father's kingdom." * * * That there is divine authority for congregational singing as an act of worship, is, in certain quarters, denied. In others, public prayer is said to be forbidden. Soon, it is to be feared, nothing will be *demanded* of us by our king: all will be "just as you like it." The body might as well be headless. Singing the praises of the God of love is called "a free-will offering," as though all worship did not flow from hearts enjoying the liberty wherewith the Son of God has made his brethren free; thankful that he has taught them *how* to pray acceptably and on what manner they may otherwise join him in glorifying his Father. If our Lord thought proper, at the request of the disciples, to dictate the "manner" of their prayers, and to make a special revelation to Paul that he might regulate the manner and the spirit of the commemorative feast, is it unreasonable that, in regard to all acts of worship, he should express his will? To some, this may be "legalistic," not, however, to those who, constrained by the love of Christ, rejoice that they are under law to him, and are free from themselves. * * * May I ask especial attention to the following "laws" for the government of congregational intercourse with God, and with each other? Col. 3: 16. 1. "Let the word of Christ dwell in you richly." 2. "In all wisdom teach and admonish one another." 3. "In Psalms, hymns, and spiritual songs, sing with grace (gratitude) in your hearts to God." * * * Here, then, we are taught congregational singing. The being to whom it is addressed, the matter of which it is composed, and the state of heart in which this spiritual sacrifice is to be offered. We have also found in Psa. 22: 22, and Heb. 2: 12, that our Lord, the head of the body, the church, is in its midst, and actually unites with it in singing praises to his Father! That, as before said, all worship must, as it were, pass through him to the Father to be accepted! Is there not, then, an ORGAN, a medium through whom acceptable worship is conveyed to God in every assembly of the saints? The eye is the indispensable *organ* that conveys to the brain the impressions made on it by visible objects; and no man cometh to God as a sinner or as a worshiper but by his Son. In saying that there is actually in every church of Christ an organ already, I do not mean one of those windy things that make "the mother of abominations" laugh at our vulgar and imbecile attempts at imitation; but a divine organ of communication between such as worship the Father in spirit and in truth, and the Father himself, in all those actions and spiritual states that are as sacrifices acceptable in and through his Son.—*Gospel Advocate,* December 29, 1886, p. 824.

6. JACOB CREATH. From this stalwart defender of the faith, we have this pointed testimony:

We must speak where the Bible speaks, and we must respect the silence of the Bible, as well as what it says, says Thomas Campbell. You have only to do this one thing, and this war of words closes forever on my part. Here I rest the controversy until you produce the apostolic example or precept for your conventions. Your conventions stand upon precisely the same footing that the one now in session in Rome does—that sects, creeds, infant-sprinkling, organ-grinding in churches, "Pastor" over "Elders" and churches stand upon, that is, as you candidly acknowledge, on the "Infer." As another advocate for all these innovations says, "They are not specially forbidden nor commanded." Neither is Romanism nor Mohammedanism. * * * Our periodicals are filled with discussions of untaught questions about organs, Missionary Societies, of which the Scriptures say no more than they do of infant rantism.—*Gospel Advocate,* 1870, pp. 566, 824.

7. BENJAMIN FRANKLIN. We will now hear the testimony of one of the greatest and most successful preachers of the nineteenth century. After spend-

ing about a half century in proclaiming the Gospel and turning thousands to the Lord, he wrote:

If any one had told us, forty years ago, that we would live to see the day when those professing to be Christians; who claim the Holy Scriptures as their only rule of faith and practice; those under the command, and who profess to appreciate the meaning of the command, to "observe all things whatever I have commanded you," would bring any instrument of music into a worshiping assembly, and use it there in worship, we should have repelled the idea as an idle dream. But this only shows how little we knew of what men would do; or how little we saw of the power of the adversary to subvert the purest principles, to deceive the hearts of the simple, to undermine the very foundation of all piety, and turn the very worship of God itself into an attraction for the people of the world, an entertainment, or amusement. * * * There would have been no conflict in the establishment of the kingdom of God, with Jews or Pagans, in bringing instrumental music in and *utilizing* it. The way was open, and it would have been one *popular element.* But did our Lord *utilize it?* No; he established his religion in a country where all worshipers, of all kinds, used instruments in worship, but *left the instruments all out!* He did not leave them out because there were not plenty of them, nor because he could not get them, nor because they were not popular; but because *he did not want them.* This is a *divine prohibition.* Neither he, nor any one of his apostles, ever used any instruments to enable them to sing; nor any one even professing to follow him, till the man of sin was fully developed, and there was a full-

grown pope. He is the gentleman to whom we are indebted for the use of the organ in worship. His fruitful mind caught the idea of *utilizing* the organ, and he took it from its more congenial place, in the theater, and consecrated it to *divine service.* * * *
If it was death under the law given by the ministrations of angels, to offer strange fire on God's altar, what may we expect for him who shall tamper with the prescribed worship in the law given by the Son of God? If death was inflicted on Uzzah for violating the law, in touching the ark of God, what shall we expect to befall the man who shall tamper with the law prescribing the worship of God? * * *
We have nothing but the common interest at stake in this matter. We cannot see an earthly interest to influence us in the course we are going. We know we are going against the current, against wind and tide; and it has been said that "he who spits against the wind spits in his own face." We are not blind to this; we know it. We know that it is not *popular*. We are perfectly aware that it is calling down on us the disfavor of many of the rich, the influential and popular; and that, on account of it, we are cut off from many amiable people, and cannot meet and worship with them. We are perfectly aware that it is against our temporal interests. We have not been, and are not, blind to all this, but have it before us, and have considered it carefully, and made up our mind to take all the consequences, and bear with meekness and patience whatever shall come. We do not court these consequences, nor desire them, but we see no way to avoid them, and maintain what we solemnly believe to be right. We, then, cheerfully accept the situation, and take the consequences, rather than give up the fullest, strong-

est and most settled conviction of our inmost soul. We cannot worship, and maintain a good conscience, *with the organ.* We are certain that we can worship acceptably *without the organ.* The friends of the organ do not doubt this.—*Gospel Preacher,* Vol. II. pp. 411, 419-423.

8. David King. We now introduce a witness from the other side of the ocean. David King was one of the strongest advocates of the restoration of the ancient order ever produced in England, and it has been said of him, by the well informed in such matters, that he "was, for many years, to England what David Lipscomb has been to this country." This certainly identifies him with the defenders of New Testament order. The following is his testimony:

"The body," or *substance,* is of Christ, and when he came and filled to the full the types and shadows of the law, they passed away in their entirety, giving place to higher institutions, by means of which the worshipers could be made perfect, and not only so, but just in proportion as these abandoned shadows are intruded into the church and worship of God they become injurious and more or less substitutes for the realities of which, in their day and place, they were the proper types and symbols. Consequently, in setting in order, by the apostles, of the church of Christ, the temple and its worship were in no degree taken as models, and this is highly reasonable, inasmuch as the existence together of the type and the antitype would be completely inadmissible. Nothing could have been easier than for the apostles to have adopted priestly, or modified priestly, vestments. There could have been no manner of difficulty in burning incense as an act of praise or worship. It cannot be supposed but that, long before the close of the apostolic ministry, they could have used and enjoined the use of instrumental music. But, no! Nothing of this sort; no trace even of a leaning, or of a desire, in that direction. The things of the shadows were done with, and those of the substance took their place.—*The Ecclesiastical Observer,* January 15, 1882, p. 16.

9. Moses E. Lard. This intellectual giant and eloquent preacher made such an impression soon after his graduation at Bethany that he was subsequently mentioned in the "Memoirs of A. Campbell" as at that early day "rapidly becoming one of the most distinguished writers and speakers in the cause" of reformation. He testifies as follows:

The question of instrumental music in the churches of Christ involves a great and sacred principle. But for this the subject is not worthy of one thought at the hands of the child of God. That principle is the right of men to introduce innovations into the prescribed worship of God. This right we utterly deny. The advocates of instrumental music affirm it. This makes the issue. As sure as the Bible is a divine book, we are right and they are wrong. Time and facts will prove the truth of this. The churches of Christ will be wrecked the day the adverse side triumphs; and I live in fear that it will do it. Our brethren are now freely introducing melodeons into their Sunday schools. This is but the first step to the act, I fear. As soon as the children of these schools go into the church, in goes the in-strument with them. Mark this.—*Lard's Quarterly,* October, 1867, p. 368.

10. DR. H. CHRISTOPHER. This cultured and scholarly man, in a vigorous and outspoken presentation of the subject, deposes as follows:

Did the Holy Spirit, then, ordain instrumental music in the church of Christ? Or did he leave it to human wisdom and prudence to determine what shall be the mode of worship so far as regards the singing? The last of these questions can never be answered in the affirmative. In the absence of certain facts, it might be inferred; in their light it may be safely denied. These facts will appear as we proceed.

The first question can be answered in the negative. Instrumental music was not used in the Jewish synagogue; and as the Christian church was modeled after it, it could not have been used in the apostolic church, unless specially ordained. The history of the church develops the fact that it was not used in any Christian assembly for several centuries after the death of the inspired men; consequently it was not ordained by the Holy Spirit in the apostolic church. * * * If, then, he did not ordain it in the church, what could have been the reason? If it were not an oversight, it must have been intentionally discarded. But it matters not with us what was the reason. We have the fact, and this, with Christians, should be all-sufficient. The fact, then, that the Holy Spirit did not. ordain instrumental music in the apostolic church is an argument conclusive that he did not design that it should be used. This fact should be with us an end of all thought and desire on the subject.   *   *   *   As a people, therefore, pretending before the world to be laboring for the apostolic purity of the church; claiming to have condemned all the corruptions and innovations which now disfigure and defile the church, and who esteem it their honor and glory, as it is, that they have proposed a greater work than that of Luther; that they will be content with nothing less than the faith and practice of the apostolic church, such a people, I take it, cannot adopt such an innovation, condemned even by themselves up to the present day, and such an instrument of corrupting and secularizing the church, without blushing at their inconsistency—without being conscious that they have abandoned their original ground and trampled under foot the great principle on which they are proceeding.   *   *   *   We are compelled to discard this innovation on primitive practice, or give up all pretension and purpose of prosecuting any further the grand design of our reformatory movement. And if we have been right up to this time, to abandon this ground and principle would be nothing less than apostasy. To this dilemma are we driven by the most remorseless logic and by the highest considerations for honesty and consistency.   *   *   *   If this opposition came from ignorant and unreasonable men, the friends of the measure might be excused for any little restiveness or impatience they might manifest under this opposition. But I submit that the opposition is neither ignorant nor unreasonable. They have always been ready to give, and have repeatedly given, the reasons which compel them to resist the introduction of this innovation.   *   *   *   I cannot, therefore, see in all my horizon one fact, argument, reason, or plea, that can justify us in using musical instruments in the worship of the church. It is an innovation on apostolic practice. This cannot be controverted. It is such an innovation, too, that prepares the way for other and equally destructive innovations. * * * Let us learn from the experience of others and be content with what God has ordained, and suffer instrumental music and all its concomitants to remain where they were born, amid the corruptions of an apostate church.—*Lard's Quarterly,* October, 1867, pp. 359, 360, 365-368.

11. W. K. PENDLETON. This distinguished educator, at one time President of Bethany College, bears significant testimony on our theme:

With respect to instrumental music, I presume that no one at all acquainted with ecclesiastical history will pretend to claim for its introduction in the church any pretense of primitive authority or warrant. * * * I am satisfied that the tendency of instrumental music is to silence congregational singing;—to usurp the place of the melody of the heart, which we are commanded "to make,"—to prevent the "edification of psalms, hymns, and spiritual songs," which is one of the social duties and privileges of the congregation, and to deliver over this part of the worship of the disciples into the artistic and often godless hands of mere amateur or hireling performers. This is the result of a careful and candid observation, for I have no prejudices against music. I love it with a love that passes expression. The grand tones of the organ lift my soul up with a power ineffably sublime. But this is not the question. We have to inquire, what is the effect of these instruments upon congregational singing? The question is a broad and practical one, and I have no difficulty in deciding it.—*Gospel Advocate,* 1889, p. 67, and *Millen. Har.,* 1868, pp. 555, 556.

12. LANCEFORD B. WILKES. This amiable and unostentatious man, whose reputation as a finished scholar and logician was fixed by his great debate with Jacob Ditzler in Louisville, Ky., was a man of strong conviction and great force of character. Writing on our theme, he says:

I fix my eyes upon the organ at its introduction into the church by, not the Lord God Almighty, but by "the Lord God the Pope," and trace its history and effects as I see them affecting churches and members of churches down to the present time, and I am constrained to pronounce the tree bad. I speak of it not out of the church, but in it. * * * The testimony of leading men of all parties is against the instrument. Even the Catholic Church, in which the god of this world is embosomed and finds his utmost quiet, furnishes occasionally a man who, rising above the spirit of his party, condemns in severe terms the instrument in the church.—*Apostolic Times,* February 3, 1870, p. 342.

13. JOHN F. ROWE. This veteran editor, though near the close of his life he indorsed the use of "a small organ" in the worship, had nevertheless previously borne this strong testimony:

There is just the same scriptural authority for the use of the organ in Christian worship as there is for the use of the mass, image worship, invocation of saints, purgatory, auricular confession, etc., in Christian worship. * * * A fearful responsibility rests upon those persons who have introduced the organ or other instruments into the spiritual worship of God. Some weak-minded people, vain and thoughtless, might be excused on the ground of ignorance; but what a terrible burden of responsibility must rest upon editors and pastors and preachers, who, knowing that the use of the organ and select choirs in the public worship is wholly unscriptural, and an invention borrowed from the carnal world, nevertheless encourage these innovations by their silent approbation, and never lift as much as the little finger of rebuke. Once we were a unit; now we are divided; who is responsible—good men or bad men, God or the devil?—*History of Reformatory Movements*, pp. 318, 322.

14. Isaac Errett. Although this distinguished editor and founder of the Christian Standard did not regard the use of instrumental music in Christian worship as wrong in itself, yet he cheerfully bore the following testimony concerning the practice:

The Standard regards it as an expedient, proposed to aid the church to perform, in an edifying way, the duty of singing; and advises against it as not necessary to that end, and as tending to create strife in many of our churches.—*Life and Times of John F. Rowe*, p. 107.

15. LEONARD F. BITTLE. This quiet and unassuming man was no less remarkable for his breadth and depth of learning than for his profound humility. By accurate scholarship and wide reading, he was well prepared to speak on the subject. He says:

The brethren whom the apostles addressed in their epistles were familiar with the Greek language, else Paul would not have written to them in this tongue. If we can find out how they understood his directions about singing, we shall know the current use of *psallo* in the primitive churches. Did the disciples of Ephesus, for instance, understand that the apostle commanded them to sing and play with the harp? or did they think he wanted them to sing without any instrumental accompaniment, and make melody with their hearts? Their uniform practice shows that they took his words in the latter sense. All reputable scholars agree that for the first three or four centuries if not for a much longer time no musical instruments were used in the churches, and that all the singing done in the worship was with the human voice alone. The use of instruments is an innovation of the Latin or Roman church, and it has been resisted by the Greek church until the present day.—*Octographic Review*.

16. THOMAS MUNNELL. This is another one of the graduates of Bethany who subsequently distinguished himself as a close student and a man of eminent ability. He left on record the following wise words on our theme:

My hope and great desire is that brethren will not insist on organs in the churches, but consider the things which make for peace and edification. We can do well without the organ, but can do nothing without harmony and love among ourselves.—*Life and Times of John F. Rowe*, p. 112.

17. John Tomline Walsh. This prominent preacher of the "Old North State," writing on "Humanisms in the Worship of God," says:

I designed saying something of worshiping God by instrumental music, but find my time and space will allow me only a word or two. If Christ has commanded us to worship in this way, or if the apostles and primitive Christians have set us the example of worshiping in this way, then it is right to do so; but if otherwise, *we must not go beyond the word of the Lord.* "Whatever you do, in word or deed, do all in the name of the Lord Jesus, giving thanks to God and the Father by Him." The Lord's day worship legitimately consists in—1. Reading the Scriptures. 2. Praise. 3. Prayer. 4. Partaking of the Lord's Supper, or breaking the loaf. 5. The Contribution or Fellowship. 6. The teaching. All these are parts of that spiritual worship which God requires at the hands of all His saints; and to omit any part is not to worship Him according to His word, or "in spirit and in truth."—*Book of Sermons* by J. T. Walsh, p. 254.

18. Dr. Robert Richardson. The distinguished author of the "Memoirs of A. Campbell" was made a member of the first Faculty of Bethany College

in 1841 and was a man of superior scholarship and ability. On the matter of maintaining the purity of the primitive faith and worship he was outspoken as will be seen from the following extract from his writings:

As it regards the use of musical instruments in church worship, the case is wholly different. This can never be a question of expediency, for the simple reason that there is no law prescribing or authorizing it. If it were anywhere said in the New Testament that Christians should use instruments, then it would become a question of expediency what kind of instrument was to be used, whether an organ or a melodeon, the "loud-sounding cymbals" or the "light guitar;" whether it should cost $50., or $500., or $1,000.; and what circumstances should regulate the performance. It happens, however, that this is nowhere said; and, consequently, no such questions of expediency can ever arise in a church that is truly and really governed by the law of the Lord.—*Life and Times of John F. Rowe,* p. 117.

19. F. G. ALLEN. This faithful preacher of the Gospel and skillful logician, founder and Editor of the "Old Path-Guide" and subsequently the Editor-in-chief of the Apostolic Guide, was a giant in debate and a strong advocate of the primitive order of worship. His editorial career was marked by many heroic efforts to defend the truth against the encroachments of error, and those who knew him well had no fears but that the cause of truth, in any

fair contest, would triumph in his hands. He deposes as follows:

I regard the use of the organ in the worship a violation of one of the fundamental principles of our plea for restoration and unity. We have ever claimed that our plea is catholic—that is, we hold as common ground that, and that only, which is conceded by all to be right. In restoring just what we find in the beginning in faith and practice, and refusing all else, we stand on undisputed ground. All partisan, disputed ground we have left to others. For instance, we immerse. All churches concede that to be baptism. It is not in debate. The controversy is all about sprinkling and pouring. That is partisan; immersion is catholic. The debate is not about what we do, but about what others do. The same is true in regard to the baptism of a penitent believer. All concede that to be right. The debate is all about the baptizing of those not believers. So of our creed, our names, our church polity, etc. All can stand where we do, for we stand on conceded ground; all cannot stand on any sectarian ground, for all cannot accept any denominational position. The grandeur and strength of this position have been the chief causes of our unprecedented growth. The world has seen and felt the advantage and self-evident correctness of this catholic position; but the introduction of the organ, since all cannot worship with it, is a violation of this grand principle. All can worship without it; all cannot worship with it. Therefore we can be united and harmonious without it; we cannot be harmonious and united with it. To introduce the organ to the destruction of our peace and unity is a complete renunciation, therefore, of this principle of catholicity characterizing our plea for the union of God's people on God's word.—*What Shall We Do About the Organ?* pp. 12, 13.

20. Dr. Winthrop H. Hopson. This eloquent pulpit orator and defender of the ancient order says:

We take the Bible, and the Bible alone, for our rule of faith; "when that speaks, we speak, and when that is silent, we are silent." Leaving all human names, all human leaders, and all human authority in religion, we follow him who said, "I am the way, the truth, and the life." When we do this we are walking in the light, and have fellowship with God, with Christ, and with one another, and the "blood of Jesus Christ will cleanse us from all sin." How very important it is that every one should ascertain for himself where the light is and walk in it!—*Sermons of Dr. W. H. Hopson,* p. 24.

21. Professor Charles Louis Loos. In harmony with the special purpose in this chapter, we continue the same line of testimony by appealing to the utterances of scholars still living; and it cannot be amiss to place at the head of this list the veteran Professor *Emeritus* of Greek in Transylvania University, Lexington, Ky. He has given utterance to much vital truth on our theme, and we quote liberally from his pen. Writing years ago on "Art-History in Churches; or, Church Æsthetics in Music," he says:

A very eminent secular paper has the following scrap of current church history, that ought not to be lost: "CHURCH CHOIRS IN COMMOTION.—The church choirs in Rochester, in this State, are in trouble. The *Union* of that city says: 'Just now there is a commotion among the choirs of some of the city churches, which extends to the congregations, growing out of high bidding for leading singers—one church bidding over another. It is said that one Presbyterian church has offered a lady who sings in an Episcopal choir the sum of eight hundred dollars per annum to change her position. In another Episcopal church the choir is being reconstructed on a basis of expending some twelve hundred per year for music. In other churches there is uneasiness in the choirs, and all are looking for something better. The church that has the most popular choir draws the largest miscellaneous audiences. One of the large churches of this city for a time had an excellent choir. Then it was overcrowded, and pewholders could not reach their seats, much less obtain them, for reason of the crowd of "run abouts" who thronged the aisles eager to hear the voluntary operatic anthem at the opening of the service. Since that choir dissolved and the prima donna went elsewhere, there is no difficulty in finding seats in the church.'" * * * The introduction of pure and high art into church worship by means of artificial machinery and its usual artistic acompaniments of operatic choirs, &c., &c., is advocated and justified on the grounds of expediency. Very well!—but remember, ye friends of policy and expediency, that antecedent reasoning, (though we feel able to meet the case even there) is not sufficient to settle such questions with us. It is the very nature of policy and expediency to be tested by *experience,* and actual experience in such things is worth more than all the finished apologetic arguments in their behalf. * * * This is really not a matter of discussion, it is a notorious *fact,* and breaks to pieces by its force all the finely woven arguments we have heard in behalf of art-worship. At one of our churches we heard this story.—By captivating arguments from policy, expediency, &c., the church was induced to introduce instrumental music. It proved finally a source of great annoyance. Often outsiders, not even always religious in any sense, had to be got to play the instruments, and others also of a similar class to sing with it. This was offensive to the religious feelings of the church. Besides, such a clique around the instrument exhibited not much reverence during preaching, prayer, and singing. *Experience* finally showed the argument for the introduction of such a help to worship to be fallacious, and the novelty that had proved an offense was put away. * * * Moreover, do we not know what an unspeakable and coveted delight to the heart of the child of God this joining in the singing of praise is? How often have we seen the humble, pious Christian man or woman strive with happy, joyful heart to unite in the hymns of the church; how often have we heard this delight expressed. Who, then, will rob these Christian hearts of this joy?—who dare rob them of this right? Yet, who does not know that the direct tendency, practically,—and, we regret to say, often the direct object *designedly,*—of art-worship, is to take away this privilege and joy from the congregation? We are not to be charged here with advocating what is bad and unedifying in the singing of congregations. If there is improvement needed, seek for it in another way; work well to improve the singing; improve and direct the living voices of the church,—and do not adopt a remedy worse in the end than the evil complained of itself. —But, before God and man, in its real good and final effects, better by far the humbler music of praise swelling up from the warm, earnest hearts consecrated to God, than the bewildering, heartless, æsthetic art-performances of organ and choir. God hears and accepts the one, as he hears and accepts the humblest prayer;—but he rejects the other, for it is a carnal offering to men's ears, and not to God. Think of it!—change the *worship of God to an attraction for men's ears!*—"pray to be heard of men" and sing to be heard of men! Sing, then, and perform sweet music for men, and give up the false pretense of making God the object. Tell men honestly that these musical church performances are, like the music on the balconies of museums, shows and theaters, to attract men, to invite patrons, and men will understand you and appreciate the performance accordingly. * * * We may be charged with making much out of a little thing. This charge is cheap, and is easily made, and generally has a ready currency among men. But we are not disturbed by such reproaches. We say what we are convinced ought to be said, and let men,—among them brethren, say what they please. The tendency to make Christianity fashionable, and carnally respectable, must be met at the cost of sneer and ridicule from any quarter.—*Millennial Har.*, 1868, pp. 280-285.

22. Professor Isaiah Boone Grubbs. This lovable man is a power in the advocacy and defense of

the truth. For thirty years he has been Professor of New Testament Exegesis and Church History in the College of the Bible, Lexington, Ky., and is a strong and vigorous writer. In the discussion of our present theme, he has contributed much that is of great value, and we take the following extracts from his gifted pen:

It should be noted that the apostle . . . compliments the disciples at Corinth for being followers of him in one important particular. "Now I praise you, brethren, that you remember me in all things, *and keep the ordinances as I delivered them to you.*" The ordinances of the Christian religion fall into two distinct classes: 1. Those to which a sinner must conform in order to become a Christian, as the confession and baptism. 2. Those by which a Christian can worship acceptably. Singing with the spirit and the understanding is an ordinance of worship; as much so as prayer and the communion. These must all be preserved as we have received them from the apostles, and nothing must be thought of as a substitute for them and nothing blended with them, that has the least tendency to neutralize their power, or formalize, secularize and carnalize our worship. Can any one with living facts staring him in the face, doubt for one moment that bleating machines in costly Christian temples are productive of this, their only effect? Why, how can it be otherwise? There sits the congregation, mute as in death. Here the godless choir and noisy fiddler fill the air with soulless strains, while the preacher, precious man, speaks his pretty piece of poetry as musically as possible by way of a solo, or as a sort of interlude.

The worship that God smiles upon is as far removed from this outward, mechanical counterfeit as his throne is from this sordid footstool. "God is spirit; therefore they that worship him *must* worship him in spirit and in truth." The soul all alive to a love all divine, gives vent to its emotions in songs and petitions that gush forth in spiritual power from the internal fountains of life. With such offerings God is well pleased. We cannot, we *will* not tolerate anything that tends to destroy this spiritual life. * * * As all things in Christian worship, as in every other department of the Christian religion, are thus to be done "in the name of the Lord Jesus," or *by his authority,* it follows that "inflexibility extends to public worship"—that its elements are fixed and determined by divine law, and that what is here done must be done by divine direction. In other words, we must adhere as rigidly to the apostolic "traditions" or "ordinances" delivered to us in this, as in every other department of the Christian religion. We then claim, as pertinent and applicable to the issue before us, the following Scriptures: "Stand fast, and hold the traditions which ye have been taught, whether by word, or our epistle." Again: "Now I praise you, brethren, that you remember me in all things, and keep the ordinances (traditions) as I delivered them to you." To these may be added, with the utmost logical propriety, the exhortation of Jude: "Contend earnestly for the faith once delivered to the saints." Grant that "Jude did not have organs or melodeons in his mind" when he said this, does the passage fail to rule them out on this account? Then if he did not also have "the mourner's bench" in his mind, it fails to rule it out! What havoc would this logic make of the word of God! And would not the Bible be a strange book if it had anticipated and specifically condemned in detail all the thousand and one innovations, in the three great departments of faith, that man in his folly might invent.—*Millennial Har.*, 1868, pp. 318, 319, 630.

23. President John W. McGarvey. This distinguished preacher and educator, who has been engaged in the systematic teaching of the Bible for more than half a century, and who is now President of the College of the Bible, Lexington, Ky., has taken a prominent and important part in the discussion of the question, and we select from his writings the following passages:

It is manifest that we cannot adopt the practice without abandoning the obvious and only ground on which a restoration of Primitive Christianity can be accomplished, or on which the plea for it can be maintained. Such is my profound conviction, and consequently the question with me is not one concerning the choice or rejection of an expedient, but the maintenance or abandonment of a fundamental and necessary principle. * * * I hold that the use of the instrument is sinful, and I must not be requested to keep my mouth shut in the presence of sin, whether committed by a church or an individual. * * * The party which forces an organ into the church against the conscientious protest of a minority is disorderly and schismatical, not only because it stirs up strife, but because it is for the sake of a sinful innovation upon the divinely authorized worship of the church; and, inasmuch as the persons

235

thus acting are disorderly and schismatic, it is the duty of all good people to withdraw from them until they repent.—It is universally admitted by those competent to judge that there is not the slightest indication in the New Testament of divine authority for the use of instrumental music in Christian worship. * * * As to the introduction of an unscriptural test of fellowship, it is enough to say that we do not refuse fellowship with those who use the organ; we only refuse to partake with them in that practice and choose to worship when we can where it is not in our way. To deny us this privilege would be an attempt to force us into fellowship with a practice confessedly unauthorized in the Scriptures, than which there could be nothing more unscriptural or more intolerant.—*In Apostolic Times,* 1881, and *"What Shall We Do About the Organ?"* pp. 4, 10.

24. David Lipscomb. As Editor of the Gospel Advocate for nearly half a century, this eminent servant of God and teacher of the Bible has taken a leading part in all the discussions pertaining to the restoration of the primitive order of work and worship and the general peace and prosperity of the church. He says:

Paul was faithful to observe the requirements of God—would do it at all hazards and under all difficulties. Nothing could deter him. Neither he nor any other apostle, nor the Lord Jesus, nor any of the disciples for five hundred years, used instruments. This, too, in the face of the fact that the Jews had used instruments in the days of their prosperity and that the Greeks and heathen nations all used them in their worship. They were dropped out with such emphasis that they were not taken up till the middle of the Dark Ages, and came in as part of the order of the Roman Catholic Church. * * * It seems there cannot be a doubt but that the use of instrumental music in connection with the worship of God, whether used as a part of the worship or as an attractive accompaniment, is unauthorized by God and violates the oft-repeated prohibition to add nothing to, take nothing from, the commandments of the Lord. It destroys the difference between the clean and the unclean, the holy and the unholy, counts the blood of the Son of God unclean, and tramples under foot the authority of the Son of God. They have not been authorized by God or sanctified with the blood of his Son. * * * The instruments were used as worship to God and to give glory and eclat to the earthly kingdom. They were tolerated by God as were many other things during this period, that he did not approve. The establishment of the kingdom itself was an act of rebellion against God. (See 1 Sam. 8: 1-20.) * * * God only has the right to prescribe conditions and ways of worshiping him. All his appointments for service and worship are revealed by the Holy Spirit, sealed by the blood of Jesus Christ, and are recorded in the Word of God. To worship him in ways not required by him is to reject God as the only Lawmaker, trample under foot the authority of the Son of God; is to count the blood of the covenant an unholy thing, and to do despite unto the Spirit of Grace. (Heb. 10: 28, 29.) * * * The introduction of the organ violates the fundamental law: ''Thou shalt worship the Lord thy God, and him only shalt thou serve.'' To use the organ is to serve some one else. ''In

237

vain they do worship me, teaching for doctrines the commandments of men." (Matt. 15: 9.) "Why, as though living in the world, are ye subject to ordinances, . . . after the commandments and doctrines of men?" (Col. 2: 20-22.)—*Queries and Answers by D. Lipscomb*, pp. 226, 227, and *Gospel Advocate*, 1899, pp. 376, 377.

25. Elisha G. Sewell. This veteran preacher, and Editor of the Gospel Advocate, has stood like a stone wall against the tide of innovation in religion. We quote the following from his pen:

Suppose that the Lord's Supper had never been required and that men had introduced it of their own accord, that it was only a human invention; then all that attend to it as a part of the worship of God would be doing just as King Saul did when he saved the best of the sheep and the oxen which he had taken from the Amalekites to make a sacrifice to the Lord, instead of destroying them. God had said nothing about a sacrifice in that case; that was altogether an invention of Saul. * * * Those who introduce instrumental music into the worship of God to-day act upon precisely the same principle as that which actuated King Saul. God commands Christians: "Let the word of Christ dwell in you richly in all wisdom; teaching and admonishing one another in psalms and hymns and spiritual songs, singing with grace in your hearts to the Lord." (Col. 3: 16.) Where God simply says "singing," men, by their wisdom and choice, put in the organ, which soon discourages and drives out singing, so far as the congregation is concerned. * * * Instruments were entirely left out of the New Testament churches, and for six hundred years or more there was not an organ in the worship of any church. The first one was introduced among the Catholics; and since then many of the leading denominations have introduced musical instruments into their churches. But there is not a word of authority for it in the New Testament. * * * David and all Israel played on instruments most zealously; he had also a new cart to carry the ark on. Neither the instruments of music nor the new cart were of God, but of David. This effort was an entire failure because David did not do the Lord's way. He afterwards called on the priests and Levites and had the ark borne on the shoulders of the Levites, as God had ordained, thus doing God's way; and the ark was borne to Jerusalem in safety. (See 1 Chron. 15.) * * * The great sin to-day in putting the organ into the worship that God ordained in the church is in presumptuously adding a purely human invention to the word of God. In so doing men pose as being wiser than God and as possessing even greater authority. The Bible must be studied as a whole, and all passages on the same subject must be examined and so applied as to make no conflict between different passages. This done on the instrumental-music question will bring harmony out of confusion and settle some very troublesome controversies.—*Gospel Advocate,* 1903, p. 532; 1907, pp. 531, 600, 601.

26. George G. Taylor. This well-known preacher and able logician strikes at the root of the matter in the following vigorous passages:

Worship, in order to be acceptable, must be offered with a view of honoring and praising the Lord, and not to please men. When in the temptation Satan sought to divert worship from its proper object, he was repulsed with the statement: "It is written, Thou shalt worship the Lord thy God, and him only shalt thou serve." (Matt. 4: 10.) * * * Now it is an undeniable fact that all that can be known of what will please the Lord in worship is what has been revealed in his word. Anything, therefore, which has not been revealed in the New Testament Scriptures can never be known to be pleasing to him; so that all such worship must of necessity be, to say the best of it, of doubtful propriety. Since all service to God must be free of doubt in order to be divinely approved (see Rom. 14: 23), and since God has nowhere in his word given any assurance that worship associated with instrumental music is acceptable with him, it must, therefore, be classed among those things which are doubtful. This being true, it follows that the condemnation which inspiration has pronounced on all services involved in doubt rests upon instrumental music in the worship of the church. * * * In the church at Rome a question had arisen concerning eating meats. Whether the meat in question was that of animals forbidden by the law of Moses or meats in general is not clearly stated; and so far as our present inquiry is concerned, it makes no difference whether it was the one or the other or neither. Some of the members of the church at Rome claimed that it was their privilege to eat meat, which others contested, strenuously contending that it was wrong and sinful for them to do so. This practice upon the part of those who doubtless honestly believed it was

240

their privilege, and which even the apostle declared was of itself innocent, became the occasion of grief to those of their brethren who entertained the opposite view. * * * Now it was the purpose of the apostle to furnish a remedy for this unhappy state of things. Looking toward the accomplishment of this benevolent design, he submitted the following statement, embodying an important principle: "The kingdom of God is not eating and drinking, but righteousness, and peace and joy in the Holy Spirit." * * * Now the state of church affairs which existed at Rome prevails at the present time among the churches all over the land. The causes producing the confusion in the two cases are in principle precisely the same, which in both instances consists in a part of the church persistently insisting on practicing what is acknowledged by them to be a simple matter of preference, while another part of the church believe and contend that such practice is wrong and sinful. The only difference between the two cases consists in the fact that the apostle admits that the specific practice in question at Rome was perfectly innocent in itself, while in the case of churches now the practices occasioning the trouble have no such apostolic concession in their favor. * * * It cannot be denied that in principle the use of instrumental music in worship now is logically parallel with eating in the church at Rome in primitive times. The kingdom of God now consists no more in the use of instrumental music than the same kingdom then consisted in eating and drinking; but it does consist in "righteousness and peace and joy in the Holy Spirit" now, just the same as it did then. * * * Many good, Christian people cannot conscientiously engage in worship attended by instrumental music even as an ''aid'' to the worship, since, on account of its objective results, they are constrained to regard it as sinful; so that when it is pressed into the service of the church under the pretext that it is only an ''aid'' to the worship, it is attended with objective results incalculably grievous. Disrupted churches, alienated affections, broken friendships, and the demolishment of Christian fellowship, with all their attendant evils, are only a few of the long list of evil consequences which brand this unholy, unlovely, unchristian, and sinful practice with the signet of divine condemnation. * * * We maintain, therefore, that divinely authorized example demands of us to dispose of instrumental music in association with church worship just as it was disposed of by the primitive churches; but by these churches it was completely and without any doubt designedly declined. This being true, conformity to this divinely established precedent requires that we also shall decline its use. All those churches, therefore, which are using instrumental music as an ''aid'' to their worship and all who advocate its use are alike in sinful rebellion against Christ.—*Gospel Advocate,* 1907, pp. 610, 611, 626, 659, 675.

27. J. B. BRINEY. This distinguished writer and debater, though subsequently identifying himself with those using instrumental music in the worship, wrote strongly and convincingly against that side in 1869, as the following extracts from his writings show:

It was a glorious day for the cause of the truth when the pious and venerable Thomas Campbell conceived and set forth the principle contained in the following language: "Where the Scriptures speak, we speak; where the Scriptures are silent, we are silent." This declaration contains the germ and pith of the present Reformation. It was the guiding star of such men as the Campbells, Scott, Stone, and Creath, in their march back to the apostolic ground. It was the watchword of those noble, grand old veterans as, weak in numbers but strong in faith, they bared their bosoms to the darts of Popery, and rushed forward to rescue the ordinances of Jesus Christ from oblivion's embrace. This was the banner that gave them possession of many a hotly contested field, and led them on to glorious victory. Under it they fought, under it they conquered, and dying, they bequeathed it to us, that under it we might at least hold what they gained. So long as we adhere to this principle may we march forward with heads erect and banners streaming. But the moment we abandon this we will be at sea, without compass or rudder, and our ship will be driven by the merciless blasts of the head winds of sectarianism in the direction of the port of Rome; and in this state of case we may well haul down our colors and seek recognition in "courts ecclesiastic." We will need the sympathy of such courts, then.

It is no matter of astonishment that, when the foregoing principle was enunciated, such a thoughtful man as Andrew Munro should make the following statement: "If we adopt that as a basis, then there is an end of infant baptism."

I beg leave to make the following respectful suggestion to Brother J. S. Lamar: If we adhere to that as a basis, then there is an end of instrumental music in the worship. But we *must* adhere to that, or else

243

the "reformation is a failure." This brings us to the main point had in view in the preceding essays. That singing as worship is a divine appointment, is abundantly clear, from the following Scriptures: "What is it, then? I will pray with the spirit, and I will pray with the understanding also. I will sing with the spirit, and I will sing with the understanding also." 1 Cor. 14: 15. "And be not drunk with wine wherein is excess; but be filled with the spirit; speaking to yourselves in psalms and hymns, and spiritual songs, singing and making melody in your hearts to the Lord." Eph. 5: 18, 19. "By him, therefore, let us offer the sacrifice of praise to God continually, that is, the fruit of our lips, giving thanks to his name." Heb. 13: 15.

Singing is worship only as it consists in prayer and praise. It is not the sound simply, the mere music, that renders it acceptable to God, but the sentiments of devotion. From the first of the above quotations we learn that in these sentiments of prayer and praise, the spirit and the understanding unite. In the third quotation these sentiments are called "sacrifice of praise," and are defined to be the "fruit of our lips." It follows, then, with the clearness of a sunbeam, that the *instruments* to be used in offering this sacrifice are the *vocal* organs with which God has endowed his creature, man. Here, then, is a divine ordinance consisting in the offering of prayer and praise to the Lord with our lips—this latter term being used generically to denote all the vocal organs.

Now, I affirm that an "instrumental accompaniment" is an *addition* to this ordinance, and affects its character, and is therefore an infringement of the divine prerogative.

That singing is worship is a divine ordinance, will not be questioned in the face of the Scripture cited above. That the "instrumental accompaniment" is an addition, is simply certain from the historical facts in the case, it having been born five hundred years out of time. Therefore, whatever men may think of its expediency, it affects the character of the divine appointment, and cannot be tolerated for a moment.

* * *

Am I told that it is expedient because "it attracts the world?" I beg leave to state that the worship of the Lord's house was not ordained for the world. Is the Church of the Lord Jesus Christ to be brought down to the standard of the world? Is this the programme of expediency? If the caprice of the world is to be regarded in these matters, the very same emergency that demands the organ will demand the very best skill in its use, and, therefore, the beer-bloated Dutchman from the theater of Saturday night will be in demand in the sanctuary of God on the Lord's day!

* * *

The Holy Spirit has provided for the use of singing in another capacity aside from the worship proper: "Let the word of Christ dwell in you richly in all wisdom, teaching and admonishing one another in psalms and spiritual songs, singing with grace (gratitude) in your hearts to the Lord." Col. 3: 16. Singing, then, may be used in teaching and admonishing. Can this be done with an instrument? Let the Spirit answer: "And even things without life-giving sounds, whether pipe or harp, except they give a distinction in the sounds, how shall it be known what is piped or harped?" 1 Cor. 14: 7.

Evidently, there is neither teaching nor admonition in inarticulate sounds. The instrument does not give the necessary distinction in the sounds. This being the case, there is no place in the assembly of the saints for the organ, and they who introduce it do so at their peril.

* * *

Having seen that the "instrumental accompaniment" is sinful, *per se,* I wish to put it upon another footing. In his first letter to the Corinthians, Paul teaches that when an enlightened Christian eats meat which has been sacrificed to an idol, his act is not sinful, *per se.* But as he clearly teaches there may be circumstances under which such an act would be exceedingly sinful. If there were those who were not so fully enlightened upon this point, and whose consciences were therefore weak, this weakness was to be the rule of action in the case. And of violating this rule the Apostle says: "But when ye sin against the brethren and wound their weak conscience, ye sin against Christ." Now, in this music affair I am willing to be called a weak brother, if thereby the cause of my Savior can be served. Indeed, I like that weakness which fears to leave the channels designated by the word of God, to try the trackless and shoreless sea of expediency. My conscience will not allow me to engage in singing as an act of worship, where there is an "instrumental accompaniment." A weak conscience, you say? Be it so, I demand that my weak conscience shall be respected. Remember, that when you introduce an organ into the worship, and thus wound my conscience, however weak it may be, you sin against Christ, and he will call you to an account for it in the great day.

Let the plain truth be told: The introduction of

the organ is no mere impropriety; it is a gross insult to the Lord Jesus Christ, and a sin against the God of Heaven. The observance of this Pauline principle will keep the instrument out while time lasts.—In *Apostolic Times,* June 10 and 17, 1869, pp. 69, 73.

28. Dr. William Thomas Moore. This distinguished preacher and author, though now fully identified with those using the organ in worship, delivered an Address in 1872 from which the *Apostolic Times,* Lexington, Ky., published an extract, and made editorial comment as follows:

We have been much edified quite recently by reading an Address by Brother W. T. Moore entitled "The Utilitarian Tendencies of the Present Age and the Remedy." It contains some remarks on organs and kindred corruptions, which we think worthy of republication. The reader will please remember that it is Brother William T. Moore, of the Central Christian Church, Cincinnati, from whom we quote, and keep this in mind while reading the following:

"Religion is not now what it once was—an earnest, deep and certain faith in the power of the gospel to convert the world, but a cold and lifeless formalism, resting on a doubtful hope in the promises of God, and almost entirely destitute of life or practical godliness. The church is no longer considered sufficient of itself to perform its mission, and hence 'auxiliaries to the church' are becoming as numerous as the locusts of Egypt. A long catalogue of human societies, bearing banners which absorb the rays of light from the church, is now occupying, if not the most prominent, at least the most conspicuous place in our moral library. But these outside appliances are considered indispensable agents to do the 'dirty work' of the church, and as such, they must be sheltered by its gracious wings. Nor does the evil stop here; for a new order of machinery has recently been brought into requisition. 'Picnics' and 'fairs,' 'pew rents' and 'door fees,' and the 'called and sent' instruments to defray the expenses of the church. The worship, too, which of all other things, should be most spiritual, largely partakes of the same principle. Prayer books for the soul's own warm and healthy outpourings. And, for that deep-toned, stirring melody in song, tempered by the love of God 'shed abroad in the heart,' we have *organs* that grind out their *quantum sufficit* by purely mechanical force! In some places they are not satisfied with the ordinary way of performing this 'praise to God,' but have clearly out-heroded Herod himself, by applying the power of steam to the instrument to make it do better and faster work!! Who ought to wonder now at the 'confessionals' and 'indulgences,' and who can fail to discern the tendencies of the age?"—*Apostolic Times,* October 10, 1872, p. 4.

The truth to which Brother Moore then gave such wise and timely utterance is still the truth, and those "tendencies" are still the same, only they have gained in momentum and are now going at a more rapid rate. Some are still making the same noble fight which he was rightly making then, and the deepening conflict is sometimes discouraging; but they know that it is impossible to estimate the good that might have been accomplished and the vast difference it might have made in the condition of things to-day, if all had faithfully persevered in the fight; and so they press on in the conflict with the sure conviction that God reigns and the truth will prevail.

CHAPTER XVI.

Making Tests of Fellowship and Causing Division.

One of the most common defects in the reasoning process as conducted by most men in all ages, is the practice of using a term in different senses in the same connection. Such reasoning is nothing short of "beating the air," and it leads to constant misunderstanding and hopeless confusion. In much of the controversy during the last quarter of a century over the question of union among Christians, and especially over the mooted question of making tests of fellowship, this defect has shown itself conspicuously, and it is still seen in the pulpit, in social conversation, in books, and in the periodical literature of the age. One speaker or writer will charge another with making some opinion or practice "a test of fellowship," while the latter replies, not only stoutly denying the charge, but turning it back in a fierce countercharge upon his accuser, alleging that the accuser himself is the one who is guilty of the thing charged. Thus, charge and countercharge follow each other in quick succession, and general confusion is the result. The truth of the matter is that, in many instances, though from different points of view and for different reasons, both sides, as we shall see, are responsible for the thing charged.

Now, that we may have no such misunderstanding and confusion in the present investigation, let us, first of all, have a clear and definite understanding as to the meaning of our terms. What, then, are we to understand, as properly meant, by making a thing *a test of fellowship?* Back of this, we should first understand what is meant, in such a connection, by the term "fellowship" itself. Certainly if those who use these terms in debate are not agreed on what the terms mean, and hence do not use them in the same sense, it is folly to be charging one another with making tests of fellowship, or to be attempting to use such terms in discussion at all.

The word "fellowship" in the English New Testament is used as a translation of the Greek word *koinonia* (κοινωνία). Hence our first duty is to ascertain whether the meaning assigned by the Greek lexicons to κοινωνία, and that assigned by the English lexicons to *fellowship,* are the same. If they are, then, if the lexicons are reliable, we shall not only know that the one is a correct translation of the other, but we shall necessarily have the idea which the two terms in common convey. According to the very highest authority, the Greek word, as defined in English, means "joint participation, intercourse;" and according to equally high authority, the English word is defined as follows:

Webster: "A state of being together; companionship; partnership; association: hence, confederation; joint interest.''

WORCESTER: ''Partnership; joint interest.''

STANDARD DICTIONARY: ''The condition of being sharers or partners; community of interest, condition, or feeling; joint interest or experience; as, *fellowship* in prosperity or adversity.''

THE CENTURY DICTIONARY: ''The state or condition of sharing in common; intimate association; joint interest; partnership; as, *fellowship* in loss.''

MARCH'S THESAURUS: ''The state of being a companion; community of interest.''

MURRAY'S NEW ENGLISH DICTIONARY: ''Participation, sharing (in an action, condition, etc.); something in common, community of interest, sentiment, nature, etc. 2. Companionship, company, society; an instance of this.''

The reader will observe that all of these authorities give substantially the same definition, and that they use very much the same language in framing their definitions. Accordingly, we see that the two terms, *fellowship* and κοινωνία, mean in common such an ''association,'' ''community,'' ''partnership'' and relation of persons as involves a ''joint interest,'' ''sharing a thing in common,'' or ''joint participation.'' Hence, it follows that, if two or more persons do not have a ''joint interest'' in a thing, ''share it in common,'' or ''jointly participate'' in it, they do not have fellowship with each other in that thing. This, from the premises before us, is self-evident. Furthermore, it follows, with equal clearness and conclusiveness, that whenever and in whatever capacity persons are so associated and related as to "share things in common," and to be "joint participators" in certain obligations and privileges, they may be said to be in fellowship with one another. We are, therefore, led to this necessary conclusion that, to *fellowship* one, means to have "joint interest" or be a "joint participator" with one in a given thing, and to *disfellowship* one, means to refuse to have such "joint interest" or "joint participation."

Moreover, according to the facts now before us, it does not follow, because one refuses fellowship— "joint interest," "joint participation"—with another in any particular thing or act, that therefore fellowship—"joint interest"—in all things and all acts is refused. In all such cases, there may be only the refusal to have fellowship with another in some special thing or act. Of course this particular act in which fellowship with others is refused may or may not be of a character to justify refusal of fellowship with them in all acts, but this would be a question to be determined strictly upon its own merits, and has nothing whatever to do with the special point of making a thing a test of fellowship, which is the only point now under discussion. A single act might so vitiate one's character as to justify withdrawal of fellowship from him, not only in the particular vitiating act, but from the person himself, as

253

such, because of his own character as affected by that act.

But, what sense must we attach to the word "test" in the phrase "making tests of fellowship?" Defining the word "test," Webster says: "Discriminative characteristic; standard of judgment; ground of admission or exclusion." Accordingly, anything which is made either a "ground of admission" to, or cause for "exclusion" from a given fellowship, is thereby, and in both instances, made a "test" of fellowship.

With this definition of terms before us, we are now prepared for the conclusion that whenever and wherever anything either *prevents* "joint participation," on the one hand, or is made a *condition* of it, on the other hand, it is thereby, and in both instances, *made a test of fellowship,* and it is made so *primarily* by those who constitute it into such a condition, and *secondarily* by those whom it thus prevents. Those constituting it into such a condition say, by their act, we will not permit "joint participation" with us, except on this condition. Those whom it prevents say, by their act, we will not have "joint participation" with others where the said condition exists. Just here we have nothing to do with the *reason* or *cause* for the course pursued by either party. Logically, this has nothing whatever to do with the naked question now before us, namely, what it is to make a thing a test of fellowship, and who does it.

It is proper, in this connection, to inquire into the class or character of things which should be made a test of fellowship. Be it observed, then, first of all, that men should make nothing a test of Christian fellowship which they do not regard as either essential or detrimental to Christian character; but, conversely, certainly whatever they do so regard should be made such a test. This statement of the case will doubtless go unchallenged; but it is utterly impossible to either think or speak intelligently and without confusion on the matter of making tests of fellowship until the fact is first clearly understood and appreciated that it may be done, as we have already seen from our definition of terms, from two very different points of view, and for very different reasons. For example, one may refuse to fellowship another as a Christian because of not regarding the latter as a Christian; or, in the case of one who is regarded as a Christian, one may refuse fellowship—"joint participation"—in a given act or course of conduct regarded as unbecoming in a Christian.

Now, it must be evident to any thoughtful mind that, while the act of making a test of fellowship occurs in both of these cases, yet the act in the two cases is superinduced by very different considerations. In the former, fellowship is withheld because those from whom it is withheld have not yet become Christians, or at least are regarded as not having become such, in which case they, of course, have to be so treated; and in the latter there is merely a refusal to participate or join in an act or course of conduct with those who, notwithstanding they are regarded as Christians, yet are guilty of conduct in this particular case which is thought to be inconsistent in a Christian. The refusal of fellowship—"joint participation"—with them in this latter case is, therefore, not necessarily a pronouncement upon their Christian character, except in so far as it is thought to be affected by the particular course of conduct in question. It merely means that one Christian cannot conscientiously join with another in an act which is thought by the former to be wrong.

In the light of these principles, let us now examine the mooted question of making instrumental music in Christian worship a test of Christian fellowship. Two questions at this point claim our attention. *First,* is it made a test of fellowship by those introducing it, by those withdrawing from it, or by both sides? *Secondly,* to the extent that guilt is involved in the case, to which side does it attach?

As to the first of these questions, that those introducing it make it a test of fellowship is so demonstrably true, that it is strange that it was ever called in question. In substance they say to others: "We will not permit you to have fellowship with us without the use of instrumental music in the worship," thus making it a "ground of admission" to fellowship, the identical thing which Webster says is a test. If stipulating a thing as an absolute *sine qua non*—an indispensable condition on which men can have fellowship in a given fraternity, and without which they cannot have it, is not making it a test of fellowship, then it is difficult to see how such a thing can be done at all.

It is a significant fact, too, that when departures from the original principles of the Restoration of the nineteenth century began first to appear, this position was openly avowed and defended by some of the ablest scholars and logicians of the time who lived and died with the same convictions. The American Christian Review, the Apostolic Times, and other religious journals were strong in its defense; and the disposition on the part of many in recent years to take the opposite position only shows how rapidly men drift with the current of apostasy when they are once loosed from their moorings. From the Apostolic Times of September 8, 1870, from an article by Brother J. B. Briney on "Who Makes the Test?" we take the following extract:

Let us suppose a case. A company of men and women, tired of sectarianism, agree to throw away all human creeds and confessions of faith, and adopt the simple worship of the New Testament. Their motto is, Where the New Testament Scriptures speak we speak; where these Scriptures are silent, we are silent. Time moves on and they are happy. But in process of time ideas of expediency and progress come in, and some of the brethren think it expedient to have an organ in the worship; and others, not viewing the question as simply one of expediency, oppose the introduction of the new element as a matter, with them, of conscience. By count, however, it is discovered that the majority are in favor of the organ. The minority protest. They say, Brethren, this is not in harmony with our original motto. The New Testament Scriptures know nothing of the organ. They are silent here. Our consciences will not allow us to worship with the new element. The others say, We have the majority. This is a question of expediency, and in all such questions the majority *rule*. The minority reply, You can give neither precept nor example for the use of the instrument. We desire to live in fellowship with the congregation in which we have seen so many happy days, but we cannot do it if you bring in the new item of worship. We regard it as unauthorized and corrupting; as calculated to carnalize the worship. But, say the majority, we have determined to use the instrument, and you can either accept that or withdraw from the congregation. Here, now, is a new test of fellowship. Who has made it? Certainly the majority, as it seems to me. They say to the brethren, ''You cannot have the fellowship of the congregation unless you accept the organ. We think more of our unauthorized instrument than we do of either your consciences or your fellowship.''

The foregoing extract, in so far as it deals with the action of those introducing the organ, is correct. In fact, thus far, it is simply unanswerable. Its author has since gone over to the side of those introducing the instrument, but his argument, nevertheless, remains irrefutable. But it does not, in our judgment, go the full length of the principle involved. Discussing this principle apart from any concrete example, we saw that when a thing either prevents fellowship, or is made a condition of it, it is thereby, and in both instances, made a test of fellowship.

It only remains to show now that, in an important sense, but from a radically different point of view, the opposing side—those whom the instrument *prevents* from entering a fellowship, also make it a test of fellowship. But in what way and to what extent do they do this? First of all, they do not do it in the sense that they will not, under any circumstances, fellowship the persons themselves who engage in the practice. Here is a distinction which is often overlooked. It is one thing to withdraw fellowship from a person, as such, but certainly a very different thing to merely decline joining with a person in an act which is held by those so declining to be wrong. So far as the principle now under review is concerned, the opposing side in the instrumental-music controversy simply decline to participate in an act which they believe to be wrong. It does not necessarily follow that they pronounce judgment upon the Christian character of those from whom they withhold joint participation in the particular act in question only in so far as they may regard that act as inconsistent in a Christian. To that extent they believe such persons are doing wrong, but just how far the wrong may vitiate the character and standing of such persons before God so as to render them unworthy of Christian fellowship at all, is a question to be determined upon its own merits, and should not be confused with the mere act of declining "joint participation" or "fellowship" with them in what is held to be wrong. Now, the way in which this latter class makes the mooted practice a test of fellowship is in the fact that their fellowship—"joint participation"—with others is made to turn precisely on this practice. In substance, they say to the other side: "Remove this practice, and we will enter your fellowship; retain it, and we will stay out." Never mind now about *why* they stay out. The reason for their act has nothing whatever to do with the point which we are now considering, namely, in what way is fellowship affected by their act?

To state the case fully and in its simplest form, it is as follows: One side says: "We will not permit you to enter our fellowship without the organ." The other side says: "We will not enter your fellowship with the organ."

As just observed, we need not mind now about the *reason* for the action of either side. It is *what* each side does, and not the *reason* for it, that we are here considering. The reason why an act is performed may have much to do with the propriety or impropriety, the innocence or guilt which the act may involve, but it can have nothing whatever to do with the mere act itself, and it is the latter which is now under review. But in a case where one side will not permit persons to enter a fellowship without the organ, and the other side will not enter that fellowship with the organ, in what way and to what extent is it thereby made a test of fellowship? It is here maintained that both sides make it such a test: the one in making it a "ground of admission" to, and the other in making it a "ground of exclusion" from, fellowship; and thus, in both cases, according to Webster's definition of terms, it is made a test of fellowship.

We are now prepared to consider the question of guilt involved in the case. To which side does guilt attach? Or, does it attach to both sides? So far as anything practical is concerned, the answer to this question turns upon the motive or motives which prompt the parties to action. If action on either side is prompted by the conviction that God cannot be pleased in the case by any other action, then those taking such action are compelled to it in order to avoid an outraged conscience. On the other hand, if action in either case is prompted by a mere preference which the parties to it believe they can waive without the Lord's disapproval, then, if they refuse to waive it, the conclusion is irresistible that all the guilt which is involved in a needless schism in the body of Christ attaches to them. There is no possible escape from this conclusion.

Now, touching the particular case in hand, those who introduce the organ in worship only claim to do so on the ground of a liberty in Christ which permits them to have it or not to have it as they may prefer. This, of course, leaves them free to have it or to dispense with it according as they may like. Hence, whatever else may be said for or against their course in any given instance, they are not, according to their own admission, shut up to any one course to the exclusion of all others. The "liberty" on which they profess to act, if they really have that liberty, permits them to dispense with the organ in worship, if they will do so, under any and all circumstances. And hence, the solemn and serious situation which confronts them is the deliberate creation and perpetuation, on their part, of division in the body of Christ in the face of the fact, according to their own admission, that they *could* prevent such division and still maintain a pure conscience before God and before man. This is assuming a fearful responsibility.

Now, on the other hand, those who oppose the organ in worship do so under the conviction that the practice is displeasing to God and that they, therefore, cannot engage in it without doing what they believe to be wrong in the sight of God. Never mind now about whether they are right or wrong in their convictions. That is not the question. Their convictions on this point may be wholly unnecessary and their judgment at fault in drawing the conclusion on which they act, but that is not the point now before us. Whether their judgment is correct or not, and whether their convictions are necessary or not, has nothing whatever to do with the fact as to what their convictions are. Every thoughtful mind is compelled to see that whatever their convictions are, they cannot be true in the sight of God and not act on them; and their convictions, in the present case, are that the use of instrumental music in the worship of God is displeasing to Him, and they are, therefore, according to all the facts in the case, compelled to refrain from it. Unlike those on the other side, these are shut up to one course, to the exclusion of all others, and they are compelled to pursue this course in order to maintain an inviolate conscience, and thus be true in the sight of God. From their point of view, and the motives prompting their course, if division in the body of Christ comes, they cannot help it. They cannot do, and the Scriptures do not require them to do, what they believe to be wrong in order to prevent division. When it comes to guarding this sacred principle, the Son of God himself said he came to send division. While division in itself is essentially wrong, it should be carefully remembered that guilt does not necessarily attach to the one who causes it. Hence, the inspired apostle does not pronounce condemnation upon Christians for merely *causing* division, but he is careful to specify the *particular way* of causing division which he condemns, and which is always and everywhere to be condemned. In his own words, it is thus expressed: "Now I beseech you, brethren, mark them that are causing the division and occasions of stumbling, contrary to the doctrine which ye learned; and turn away from them," Rom. 16:17.

Thus, it will be seen that the words, "contrary to the doctrine which ye learned," constitute the divine criterion by which to determine when causing division is wrong, and when it is not. When men cause division by urging what God has taught and requires, they do right; when they cause it by urging what God has not taught and does not require, they do wrong. In view of this principle, our Savior said: "Think ye that I am come to give peace in the earth? I tell you, Nay; but rather division," Luke 12:51. Of course this only means that He came to cause division in cases where some accept His teaching, and others depart from it. Hence, to cause division *according to* "the doctrine"—that is, by urging what the doctrine requires, is right; but to cause it *"contrary to* the doctrine"—that is, by urging what the doctrine does not require, is wrong.

Finally, according to facts unanimously admitted by all parties on both sides, the case now before us stands thus: One side introduces a practice admitting that the Lord does not require it, and knowing, in advance, that division in the body of Christ will be the inevitable result; the other side refuses to engage in the practice believing that the Lord requires them to stand aloof from it. Hence, here is an instance of division in the body of Christ mutually caused by both sides in a case of two opposing parties, but with this radical difference, viz., it is caused by one side when there is not only no necessity for it, but the most solemn of all reasons against it; while it is caused by the other side when there is not only a stern necessity for it, but when it is the last resort in order to maintain a pure conscience toward God and toward man. In the latter case, innocence can be maintained in no other way; in the former, only guilt is incurred.

CHAPTER XVII.

An Appeal to the Candid and Reflecting.

To all the candid and reflecting of every name and creed, but most especially to those who profess no creed but the Bible, this Appeal is respectfully and fraternally addressed. It is taken for granted that the well-informed of this class already deplore the divided condition of the church of God, and would rejoice at the restoration of union, harmony, and peace among its members. It is further assumed that all candid and reflecting persons, whether well-informed or otherwise, are prepared to give respectful attention to any reasonable arguments which concern either the cause or the cure of this baleful condition.

This Appeal is purposely limited to the class here named, for the simple reason that it is useless to appeal to any others. Those who are committed to a given course regardless of either reason or consequence, are, as a rule, not prepared to treat with proper courtesy or to listen with due patience and respect to any argument or appeal from those who differ from them, no matter how serious nor how just may be the ground for such argument and appeal.

But there are multitudes of honest and sincere people who are involved in error on what constitutes divinely acceptable worship, and who occupy their present position simply because they have always been under circumstances which veiled from their eyes the true position. Such persons are always more or less open to conviction, and are ready to renounce error and to walk in the light of the truth as it may dawn upon their pathway. It is not unreasonable to hope that a courteous, respectful, and fraternal appeal to this large class will not be wholly in vain.

For the sake of clearness and conciseness, it is proposed to present the facts and arguments of this Appeal under the two following heads: 1. Its object. 2. The means necessary to its accomplishment. We shall, therefore, briefly consider, first of all:

I. The Object of Such an Appeal.

The reader is entitled to full and adequate information on this point. No child of God, no matter how grossly involved or thought to be involved in error, can consistently be asked, on this account, to make any change in his religious position without the definite and well-grounded assurance that the new position to which he is invited will not only involve no greater error than the one in which he is already supposed to be involved, but that the end in view is one which demands such a change.

Happily for us, the end which is sought in the

present case is one which will commend itself to all right-thinking persons. That end is nothing more nor less than the union and coöperation of all the children of God upon a basis which is not only not called in question by any one, but which all accept as authorized by the Holy Scriptures. Surely this transcendently great and praiseworthy object not only merits the serious attention of my readers, but also any possible effort on their part in bringing about a consummation so devoutly to be wished.

That we may the better appreciate the importance of an Appeal with such an end in view, let us dwell, for a moment, on the religious situation which now confronts us. Among all the facts of the religious world of to-day, none, perhaps, is more prominent than the fact of division. Not only are there different denominations, as they are popularly styled, but often the same denomination is divided and subdivided into warring factions and parties. It is true, much is heard nowadays to the effect that the spirit of union is "in the air," and wherever it is so, we should, of course, thank God for it; but, nevertheless, the fact of division still remains, and with it a strange unwillingness, in many quarters, not only to have one's faith and practice in general subjected to the light of investigation, but an equal unwillingness to surrender matters which even their advocates themselves regard as matters of pure indifference. This only blocks the way to union and serves to perpetuate the babel of denominationalism with its multifarious contradictions and inconsistencies which have been the bewilderment of men for centuries, reminding one of Milton's graphic lines:

> A universal hubbub wild
> Of stunning sounds and voices all confused.

Paul's picture of the Corinthian factions, crying "I am of Paul; and I of Apollos; and I of Cephas; and I of Christ," is vividly reproduced on a vastly extended scale, and the work of strife and rending the body of Christ continues. Indeed, it may be truly said that, as the enemies of Christ mangled His physical body and nailed it to the cross, so the professed friends of Christ have divided His spiritual body and left it bleeding at every pore, while insidious skepticism and infidelity are spreading their deadly poison and sapping the foundation of religious faith. When the Master prayed for the oneness of His followers, He put it in this form: "that they may all be one; even as thou, Father, art in me and I in thee, that they also may be in us; that the world may believe that thou didst send me," (Jno. 17: 21). Precisely as it is here distinctly implied that union among the followers of Christ will establish and strengthen the faith of men in the divine origin of His cause, so, beyond all question, division in the body of Christ is one of the most powerful weapons ever wielded by infidelity against that cause. Hence, the object of this Appeal is to increase the number of those who delight to sing:

Let party names no more
The Christian world o'erspread;
Gentile and Jew, and bond and free,
Are one in Christ their head.

II. The Means Necessary to Its Accomplishment.

It is the purpose here simply to indicate such steps as are necessary to the end in view, and these may be considered in the following order:

1. It is impossible, of course, to effect union between two parties without one of them yields to the other. This settles it, then, that there can never be union between the advocates and the opponents of instrumental music in the worship until one side yields to the other, or both sides yield in common. This latter is the proper course to pursue if it can be pursued without the sacrifice of truth or conscience on either side.

2. Concerning the two parties to this baleful controversy, which one of them, if either, should yield to the other? Or, is it a case in which each can yield to the other, and thus by mutual concession effect the desired union? This would seem to be the charitable and magnanimous course for both sides, and I hesitate not to say that, in all cases where it is possible to make such mutual concession without any sacrifice of truth or conscience, it ought to be made—yea, and it *will* be made by all well-informed persons who have the Spirit of Christ. One of the primary and fundamental principles of all Christian

living is the principle of mutual consideration and mutual forbearance; while, on the other hand, another principle for the regulation of Christian conduct, equally vital and fundamental, is the obligation to refuse to yield wherever either truth or conscience would be violated by the act.

Now, the author of this Appeal would not ask either side in the present case, nor in any other case, to yield to any extent whatever at the expense of such a sacrifice. And this brings us face to face with the one vital question now at issue, viz., what are the limits within which men may properly be called upon to surrender any practice in religion? Or, to vary the question, where is the line, drawn by the pen of Inspiration, up to which men may yield in religious matters, but beyond which they cannot yield? If this line can be definitely located, we can then know, beyond the shadow of a doubt, what should be our course toward the use of instrumental music in the worship of God, and we can know this regardless of which side of the line this practice may be found to be on, the only essential point being that we either can or cannot surrender the practice according as it is found to be on the one or the other side of the line. As we are dealing purely with matters of casuistry at this point, Paul's principle shall be our guide in locating the line in question: "To him who accounteth anything to be unclean, to him it is unclean;" and again: "Whatsoever is not of faith is sin," Rom. 14: 14, 23. Observe that this

271

principle takes no note of whether a given thing is wrong in itself or not. It only considers an act in the light of how it is viewed by the actor regardless of whether that view is correct or not. The act or course of conduct may be right in itself, but if the actor believes it to be wrong, to him it is wrong, and God requires him to refrain from it. In the language of Hodge on the passage: "If a man thinks a thing to be wrong, to him it is wrong."

Now, in the light of this Pauline principle, the conclusion is inevitable that, so far as moral consistency is concerned, while men *may* always either do, or refrain from doing, an act when they do not believe that their course in either case would be sinful, nevertheless they *must* always do, or refrain from doing, an act when they believe that the opposite course in either case would be sinful; and this locates the line and fixes the limits within which men may properly be asked to surrender a religious practice.

Now, in order that we may see the proper application of these principles to the use of instrumental music in Christian worship, we here note the facts in connection with the practice. Detailed discussion of them is unnecessary at this point, and we shall be content, in the main, merely to state the facts, which are as follows:

1. It is a fact that the church of God is divided. The unholy condition meets men wherever they go.

2. It is a fact that it is divided over the use of instrumental music in the worship.

3. It is a fact that the Bible condemns division. It condemns it in the strongest terms. In His great intercessory prayer, the Son of God anticipated it, and thus addressed the Father: "Neither for these only do I pray, but for them also that believe on me through their word; that they may all be one; even as thou, Father, art in me, and I in thee, that they also may be in us: that the world may believe that thou didst send me," Jno. 17: 20, 21. Paul the Apostle said: "Now I beseech you, brethren, through the name of our Lord Jesus Christ, that ye all speak the same thing, and that there be no divisions among you; but that ye be perfected together in the same mind and in the same judgment," 1 Cor. 1: 10.

4. It is a fact that those who introduce instrumental music into the worship of God can worship Him with a clear conscience without its use. They themselves admit this, and have always admitted it.

5. It is a fact that a part of the church cannot worship with a clear conscience with instrumental music in the worship. Never mind now about those who are accused of being "bitter" in their opposition, "factious," "hard-headed," "unreasonable," "stubborn," and "self-willed." It is here admitted that this charge is too sadly true in some instances, but we respectfully remind the reader that it does not touch the point here before us, inasmuch as such do not constitute the class on whose account this Ap-

peal is made. On the contrary, among those for whom we plead are some of the wisest, purest, most reasonable, most unselfish, and most pious persons who have ever named the name of Christ. They are intelligent, well educated, and well informed in the Bible, and they are actuated by the sincerest and strongest convictions. They simply cannot use instrumental music in the worship of God without doing violence to their consciences. They solemnly believe that the practice is displeasing to the Lord and condemned by Him. This makes it a very serious case with them.

On the other hand, they readily concede that many of those who engage in the practice are equally pious, intelligent, well educated, and well informed in the word of God, and they engage in it, as they themselves allege, because they believe it is their liberty to do so, though they do not claim that God requires them to do it. Herein is a vital and radical difference between the respective claims of the two parties. Those engaging in the practice, do so because they believe it is their liberty, though frankly admitting that God does not require it of them. This makes the case on their part easy of management; but those who refrain from the practice, do so, not because they believe it is their mere liberty to refrain, but because they believe God requires it of them. This makes the case on their part difficult of management. They are shut up to one course which they are compelled to follow, or be untrue to their consciences and to their God.

6. In view of this situation, it is a fact that this latter class *cannot consistently yield at this point,* and we respectfully add that they should not be asked to do so.

7. In view of the same situation, it is a fact that the former class *can consistently yield at this point,* and surely it is not too much to ask them to do what they can do with a clear conscience before God and man when peace, union, and harmony in the church of God are depending upon it.

Will not all the candid and reflecting carefully and prayerfully consider these facts?

More than forty years ago, when the spirit of innovation first began to show itself among those pleading for the restoration of the ancient order, and a few churches had introduced this practice, Dr. H. Christopher made a similar Appeal to the brethren at large urging them to lay it aside with all other corruptions of New Testament order, and he uttered the warning that, if this were not done, other innovations would be certain to follow. Present-day divisions, dissensions, and discussions over innovations hitherto undreamed of, are a verification of his words. I give my readers the benefit of a quotation from his strong Appeal:

As a people, therefore, pretending before the world to be laboring for the apostolic purity of the church; claiming to have condemned all the corruptions and innovations which now disfigure and defile the church, and who esteem it their honor and glory, as it is, that they have proposed a greater work than that of Luther; that they will be content with nothing less than the faith and practice of the apostolic church, such a people, I take it, cannot adopt such an innovation, condemned even by themselves up to the present day, and such an instrument of corrupting and secularizing the church, without blushing at their inconsistency—without being conscious that they have abandoned their original ground and trampled under foot the great principle on which they are proceeding. * * * We are compelled to discard this innovation on primitive practice, or give up all pretension and purpose of prosecuting any further the grand design of our reformatory movement. And if we have been right up to this time, to abandon this ground and principle would be nothing less than apostasy. To this dilemma are we driven by the most remorseless logic and by the highest considerations for honesty and consistency. * * * If this opposition came from ignorant and unreasonable men, the friends of the measure might be excused for any little restiveness or impatience they might manifest under this opposition. But I submit that the opposition is neither ignorant nor unreasonable. They have always been ready to give, and have repeatedly given, the reasons which compel them to resist the introduction of this innovation. * * * I cannot, therefore, see in all my horizon one fact, argument, reason, or plea, that can justify us in using musical instruments in the worship of the church. It is an innovation on apostolic practice. This cannot be controverted. It is such an innovation, too, that prepares the way for other and equally destructive innovations. * * * Let us learn from the experience of others and be content with what God has ordained, and suffer instrumental music and all its concomitants to remain where they were born, amid the corruptions of an apostate church.—*Lard's Quarterly,* October, 1867, pp. 365-368.

There has been no time since the utterance of these earnest words over forty years ago when they were not applicable to the existing condition of things, and they are equally applicable to-day. We commend them to all the candid and reflecting.

Finally, the reasonableness of this Appeal, as it appears to the author, is clearly established by the fact that it asks for the surrender of nothing in the way of truth or principle, nor that men do anything otherwise in violation of conscience, but that they merely give up a practice which they themselves admit they can give up without displeasing God, and in which they know others cannot engage without a violation of conscience. Is it asking too much of men to urge them to take such a step when union, harmony, and peace among the children of God are depending upon it? Yea, ought they not gladly seize the opportunity? In the language of Thomas Campbell: "What a pity that the kingdom of God should be divided about such things!" And still further in the language of the same great man: "Who, then, would not be the first among us to give up human inventions in the worship of God, and to cease from imposing his private opinions upon his brethren, and that our breaches might thus be healed?"—*Memoirs of Elder Thomas Campbell,* p. 39.

This is the one divine pathway, and the only pathway, that leads to the union for which the Lord prayed, and for which the Apostles pleaded; and it is to this infallibly safe pathway, in the light of all the facts presented from divers fields of evidence throughout this volume, that the present Appeal humbly invites all the candid and reflecting. It is still true that "if we walk in the light, as He is in the light, we have fellowship one with another and the blood of Jesus His Son cleanseth us from all sin," 1 Jno. 1: 7. This divine cleansing and this holy fellowship are open to all who are willing to walk in the truth.

GENERAL INDEX.

A.

Ado, 3.

Alderman, 40.

Alford, Henry, 195.

Allen, Frank G., 227.

Allen, Thomas M., 211.

Altar, golden, 112.

Alzog, 162.

Ambrose, 118-133.

American Cyclopedia, 139, 152.

American Revision Committee, 86.

Animal, 72.

Animosity, 34.

Apostolic example and instrumental music, 98.

Appeal, an, to the candid and reflecting, 266; object of such an, 267; means necessary to the accomplishment of the, 271.

Aquinas, Thomas, 176.

Auricular confession introduced before instrumental music, 3.

B.

Bagster, 11.

Bagster's Hebrew-English Lexicon, 96.

Baptizo, water does not inhere in, 65, 67.

Begg, James, 60.

Begging the question, 64.

Beveridge, William, 179.

Beza, Theodore, 194.

Bias, theological, not always overcome by scholarship, 69.

Biblical Encyclopedia, on Eph. 5: 19 and Col. 3: 16, 156.

Bingham, Joseph, 125, 137, 169.

Biped, 72.

Bittle, Leonard F., on psallo, 54, 93, 225.

Briney, J. B., omitted " in the New Testament " from Thayer's definition of *psallo*, 53; claims that Peter and John worshiped in the temple where instruments were used, 99; on *ode*, 110; against instrumental music in the worship, 242; on " who makes the test? " 257.

279

GENERAL INDEX.

Dunbar, 11.
Dryden, John, 63.
Dryer, George, 171.
Dwight, Benjamin W., on change of meaning incident to words in a living language, 28.

E.

Ellicott, Charles John, 185.
Encyclopedia Britannica, 155.
Erasmus (Desiderius), 190.
Errett, Isaac, 224.
Eusebius, 122, 158.
Expedient, no human, should be adopted that causes strife, 207.
Expositor's Greek Testament, 185.

F.

Faith, matters of, 199, 207.
Fall, Philip S., 212.
Fanning, Tolbert, 206.
Fellowship, a test of, 251; definition of, 252.
Fisher, George P., on the Jewish synagogue, 141, 163.
Floruit, 18, 46.
Franklin, Benjamin, 215.
Fessenden's Encyclopedia, 155.
Fuerst's Hebrew and Chaldee Lexicon, 94.

G.

Generic commands, 71.
Gesenius' Hebrew and English Lexicon, 95.
Gieseler, Johann Karl Ludwig, 165.
Girardeau, John, 177, 196.
"Go" a generic command, 71, 77.
Gopher wood, God commanded Noah to make the ark of, 75.
Greek language, the periods of the, 18.
Green, Thomas Sheldon, 14.
Greenfield, W., 12.
Groves, 10.
Grubbs, Isaiah Boone, 232.
Guericke, Heinrich Ernst Ferdinand, 162.
Guilt, on whom rests the, for schism in the body of Christ? 261.

281

GENERAL INDEX.

H.

Hamilton, 13.

Harps, the, and harpers of Revelation, 108.

Hase, Karl August, 165.

Hatch, Edwin, 20.

Haweis, Hugh Reginald, 83.

Hawkins, Sir John, 120-123, 151.

Hetherington, William, 172.

History, not a fact in all, touching the meaning of *psallo* that justifies instrumental music in the worship, 7.

Hodge, 272.

Homan, Editor, omitted "in the New Testament" from Thayer's definition of *psallo*, 54.

Hopson, Winthrop H., 229.

Humneo, 4.

Humphreys, Frank Landon, 150.

Hurst, John Fletcher, 166.

Hymnos, 4.

I.

Idiot, 37.

Incense, 112.

Infant baptism introduced before instrumental music. 3.

Instrumental music in the worship, the introduction of, caused division and strife among the Jews, 136; those who oppose refuse to participate with those using it, 259.

J.

Jahn, Johann, 176.

Jewish Encyclopedia, 138.

Jews, strife and contention among the, over the introduction of instrumental music into their worship, 136.

Johnson, J. T., 204.

Johnson's Universal Cyclopedia, 154.

Joint participation, 254.

Jones, William, 170.

Justin Martyr, 121, 192.

K.

King, David, 218.

Kithara, 115, 116.

282

General Index.

Pressense, Edmond de, 168.

Prevent, 34.

Psallo, 4; as defined by the lexicons, 6; variety of meanings given
to the word, 14; conceded that, once meant to make instrumental music, 15; summary of definitons of, by lexicons, 16;
underwent several changes in meaning, 48; with a significant
parallel, 62; instrumental music not inherent in, 64; in the
Septuagint, 85; why did not the translators of the Bible
translate, " to play a stringed instrument with the fingers? "
88; in primary sense had no reference to music, 93.

Psalmos, 4, 189.

Q.

Quadruped, 72.

R.

Resent, 32.

Revisers of the Scriptures all belonged to religious bodies using
instrumental music in the worship, 87.

Richardson, Robert, 226.

Riddle, J. E., 160.

Ritter, Dr. Frederic Louis, 144.

Robertson, James Craigie, 170.

Robinson, 9, 21, 69, 114.

Rogers, Samuel, 210.

Rowe, John F., 223.

S.

Sayce, A. H., on change of meaning incident to words in a living
language, 28.

Schaff-Herzog Encyclopedia, 140, 152.

Schaff, Philip, 169.

Scholarship sometimes overcome by theological bias, 69.

Scope of divine command authorizing music in the worship of
God, 71.

Scott, Walter, on change of meaning in words, 31.

Scott, Sir Walter, 62.

Senses, using a term in different, 250.

Septuagint, 85-97.

Sewell, Elisha G., 238.

Trench, Archbishop, on change of meaning incident to words in a living language, 29.

Tune, pitching the, is authorized by the command to sing, 81.

U.

Union, the spirit of, "in the air," but the fact of division still remains, 268; between two parties cannot be affected without one yields to the other, 270.

V.

Vaughan, Charles John, 166.

Vincent, Marvin R., 182.

W.

Waddington, George, 171.

Walsh, John Tomline, 226.

Webster, 251.

Wilkes, Lanceford B., 223.

Winer, George Benedict, on the change the Greek language underwent, 41.

Worcester, 252.

Words, change of meaning in the history of, 26-44.

Wright, M., 12.

Y.

Yonge, 12.

Z.

Zamar, 91, 92, 93, 94, 95.

INDEX TO SCRIPTURES.